IN
SEARCH
OF
FAITH

Profiles of

Biblical Seekers

HOWARD W. ROBERTS

The Pilgrim Press

Cleveland, Ohio

DEDICATION

With gratitude to the fellow seekers
of Ravensworth Baptist Church
who listened carefully,
reflected thoughtfully,
and responded faithfully
to the ideas expressed in these pages.

The Pilgrim Press, Cleveland, Ohio 44115
www.pilgrimpress.com
© 2000 by Howard W. Roberts
All rights reserved.

Roberts, Howard W., 1947–
    In search of faith : profiles of biblical seekers / Howard W. Roberts.
        p.   cm.
    Includes bibliographical references.
    ISBN 0-8298-1412-4 (alk. paper)
    1. Bible—Biography   I. Title.
BS571.5.R63   2001
220.9'2—dc21
                                    2001021113
                                    CIP

CONTENTS

Preface . . . . *vii*

1   Seeking a Place *1*

2   Seeking Blessing *13*

3   A Tricky Seeker *25*

4   A Suffering Seeker *37*

5   A Rejected Seeker *49*

6   Seeking Sense in the Nonsense . . *59*

7   Seeking Security *71*

8   A Pushy Seeker *79*

9   A Short Seeker *87*

10   An Ambivalent Seeker *97*

11   A Questioning Seeker *109*

12   A Seeking Businesswoman *121*

13   An Ethiopian Seeker *129*

14   A Night Seeker *141*

15   The Seeker Behind All Seekers . . *153*

Notes *162*

Bibliography *165*

PREFACE

I am continually intrigued by the biblical story and the stories contained within it. I have found it most helpful to examine these stories within the story. Through my examination I have discovered that my story intersects with these stories at various places. Then, these stories become my teachers and often become a part of my story. Through the chapters of this book I will examine different seekers from the biblical material. I invite you to enter the story of the seeker who is the focus in each chapter. I hope this will be a learning and growing experience for you. It has been for me as I have prepared this material. I trust I will continue to learn and grow as I revisit these stories from time to time.

Reference to portions of the biblical material as stories creates problems for some people. For some the word *story* may indicate that this part of the Bible is not being taken seriously. Part of our difficulty with stories from the Bible stems from how we view a story in modern western civilization. Primarily, what we ask of a story today is that it entertain us or allow us to escape reality for the time being. Often readers do not expect or want to be instructed by stories they read. In ancient times, the meaning of a story was as important as its entertainment value.

In biblical times the stories were one of the principal vehicles for the transmission of ideas. Long before computers, typewriters, printing press, or handwritten books, people told stories to share information, ideas, and instructions, and to pass on traditions. Many stories were told to explain the origin of things—places, names, customs, and tribal characteristics. As people sat around the campfire someone would ask, "Why doesn't everybody speak the same language?" Then, someone would tell the story of the tower of Babel that since has been recorded in the book of Genesis.

The original tellers of these stories had two attitudes toward the stories they heard and told. First, they assumed that the story being told was based upon an actual event, but it was a story still, and thus subject to all the changes and distortions that the countless retelling of any story entails. Second, they assumed that the historical reliability of the story was of secondary importance. What really counted was what the story meant.

My purpose in the following pages is to explore several of the stories of biblical characters who were seekers. They were seeking God. Many of them responded positively to God. The biblical material is not conclusive about some of them. The searches by some of these people became watersheds for later seekers. For example, Abraham's search resulted in a clear understanding of radical monotheism. Ruth's seeking and searching challenged the notion that God's love and acceptance were tied to racial purity. Job's search called into question from that time forward the belief that God caused everything to happen, good and evil. Hosea's search resulted in the use of lovers as an analogy of the way God and human beings relate. Hosea also demonstrated that God is the seeker behind all seekers. Peter portrayed the struggle that many experience in confronting racism. The seeking of the Ethiopian eunuch challenges our narrow exclusiveness and opens us to the broad inclusiveness of God.

Explore with me these stories and others through these pages. Allow yourself to be a seeker as you read. May part of your seeking be to consider where your story and each of these stories intersect. May those intersections be places where you seek God and discover that already God is seeking you. May the reflective questions at the end of each chapter stimulate your seeking and searching. May you join fellow seekers past and present as you grow in faith. May you catch a glimpse of how many brothers and sisters you have.

Howard W. Roberts

1

SEEKING A PLACE

GENESIS 12:1–9

ANY TRIP WE TAKE has lots of intersections we must negotiate. We must decide which route to take. Of course, the route we choose is determined by where we want to go. In *The Wizard of Oz* Dorothy asked the scarecrow for directions. The scarecrow asked Dorothy where she wanted to go. Dorothy replied, "I don't know," to which the scarecrow responded, "Then it doesn't matter which direction you go, does it?" Often we don't know where we are going or where we want to go. When this is true, it doesn't matter which direction we choose.

Several years ago my son and I were riding in the car when he popped the question, "Dad, why do some people, when they grow up, get an apartment and move away from home?" I responded with what I thought was a reasonable, logical explanation about why people want to be on their own, make their own decisions, and have a place of their own. Brandon thought about my comments briefly and then said, "I think I'll just stay with you and Mom." An appropriate response for a seven-year-old, don't you think? But what about for a twenty-five-year-old or a forty-year-old? By the time Brandon was eighteen, he was buying his own house and "moving away from home."

What about leaving home? Is it necessary? What is the meaning of leaving home? If leaving is necessary, when is the right time? Does it involve a leap of faith? Does the Bible offer any help or suggestions?

The biblical material says Abraham was seventy-five when he left home. Is there any help for us in what Abraham did or when he did it? If we waited until we were seventy-five to leave home, only a handful of us would ever leave. However, according to the biblical material Abraham lived to be 175. That means that seventy-five was roughly 43 percent of his life. Seventy-five in Abraham's life was the equivalent of twenty-five to thirty in our lives, given our current age expectancy. Isn't this about the age when many people leave home today—emotionally and financially?

We are not told when or why Abraham left his home. We don't know when or how or why he got the idea that God wanted him to leave his country, his relatives, and his dad's home and venture out into the unknown, toward a land, a place that God would give him. While Abraham's ancestral roots were planted in Ur of the Chaldees in Babylonia, if the biblical account is in some semblance of chronological order, then Abraham left his father's home in Haran in Canaan to move on to the place God would show him. Earlier, Abraham had left Ur with his father, Terah, and they had settled in Haran. When Abraham was seventy-five, he left his place in Haran in search of his new place, the place that God would show him. Abraham was seeking a new place.

Paul Tournier has suggested that each of us finds a place in life, becomes secure in that place, and then leaves that place for a new place. A leap of faith is required to leave one place for another and can be compared to the performance of a trapeze artist. The trapeze artist swings on a bar high above the ground and, at the right moment, leaves one bar and reaches for another, but for a moment is between bars. This is what Paul Tournier identifies as the leap of faith.

Abraham left the security of his father's home, the support of the relatives in his extended family, and the familiarity of many known quantities in his life. Abraham left home, and in leaving home he traded the familiar for the unfamiliar, the known for the unknown, the certain for the uncertain, and the comfortable for the uncomfortable.

Leaving home was a major intersection for Abraham to negotiate. Leaving home for Abraham had a physical dimension, but much more involved and significant than the physical leave-taking was the emotional/spiritual journey of independence that Abraham set out on. This same dynamic is at work today. One person may leave home, move out of the house where she lived with her parents, move into a house next door, and be clearly described as having left home. Another may move across the continent but not really leave home.

Leaving home requires us to shift some of our dependence on other people to independence. There are some benefits of dependence. After all, someone else can be responsible for the decisions of life, receiving the blame or credit for those decisions. But a major liability is that a dependent person never really develops a self, an identity that is clearly and uniquely one's own. We need to look around at life as we give serious thought to leave-taking. We will have to give up some things like having others always take care of us. But we also will be able to take up some things like making decisions, being in charge of our lives, venturing out into the unknown, and being thrilled by the challenge of sailing in uncharted water. Life for many of us began in homes where our every need was met. And that kind of dependence is appropriate for infants who cannot look out for themselves or take care of themselves. One of the major tasks of parents is to guide their children to grow out of dependence on them into dependence on God and interdependence with them and with others.

Have you heard how eaglets learn to fly? The mother eagle takes them on her back from the nest and flies away with them.

Then, she drops out from under them and they struggle to learn to fly. She watches with her "eagle" eye to see how each is doing. As each has difficulty, she flies under it and catches it on her back, and then drops out from under it again. She repeats this process until her eaglets learn to fly and thus weans her young away from dependence on her for their survival. Parents are partners with God in guiding their children to learn how to be interdependent with other people and dependent on God.

There are those who do not want to leave home and will not. Like the eaglets, they seem never willing to try their wings on their own. Healthy parents are those who can help their children leave home, difficult though that might be. One man approached the process this way. His son had gone to college and received a good education, all of which his parents had provided for him. After graduating from college he returned to his parents' home, moving all of his things back into their house. His dad said to him straightforwardly, "Your mother and I have provided a place for you to grow up. We've made sure you got a good education. We gladly paid for all of your college expenses. Now it is time for you to be on your own. You have two weeks find a job and a place to live." Amazingly, the son had a job and an apartment within the two-week time period.

Professor Edward Wimberly has noted how things are a bit different for those entering young adulthood now and seeking to leave home. He comments,

> For socioeconomic and emotional reasons, many African American and Caucasian young adults are postponing entrance into full participation in the major tasks of young adulthood. I have heard many comments by parents of young adults between the ages of eighteen and thirty, wondering when their children will finally leave home and establish their own lives. Although it is an expectation of American culture that

young adults leave home and begin to make their own way in society, these expectations are being altered by the reality of what some are now calling the "postponed generation." Many young adults feel ill equipped emotionally to face the world. Many feel they do not yet have all the resources from the parental home needed to negotiate in the world.[1]

Usually there is a time of strong independence when a person is in resistance and/or rebellion to anything the parents have to say or suggest. This is when one should decide what it means to leave home and what direction life is going to take. That is a difficult intersection to negotiate in life. The religious dimension often is seen starkly late in high school years or just after high school, especially if the family has been actively involved in the life of a congregation. The young person physically leaves home, but is still at home emotionally and financially. Participation in the life of the church takes a long vacation. Why? The faith of the family, particularly the parents, is not the faith of the child. The one who is leaving home must decide the faith issue for him- or herself. By stopping and looking the person leaving home is better able to listen to the voice of God calling him or her to take the leap of faith. Like Abraham that person experiences the promise of God in a relationship that begins then and there and develops and expands throughout life.

People leave a lot behind that was part of home. There is usually a healthy removal of excess baggage. Some of what they leave they discover later they would like to have, but it is hard to sort all that out during the leave-taking. Our tendency is either to take everything with us or to leave everything behind, but the sorting and deciding and the choosing to take some things and leave others is vital in the process of leaving home.

Leave-taking affects the person leaving as well as those who are left. When the leaving is to go to something, the process is easier for the person leaving. When the leaving is to go from something, the process may be easier for those being left. But leaving takes its toll on all the relationships involved.

Some people leave home without realizing the significance of what is happening. For some it is a gradual easing away. For others a particular event causes a sharp, distinct break. Physically and emotionally I left home when I entered college. I did not know that anything significant was happening until we had carried my things into the college dormitory and, as my parents started to say good-bye, my mother began to cry. I was surprised. As it turned out I returned to my parents' home for Thanksgiving, Christmas, spring break, and the following summer. I bought a car that summer and drove myself to college in the fall. By the time I returned to college in the fall of my sophomore year, I had left home. I discovered a broad, expansive, unique world out there beyond home. The breadth, expansiveness, and uniqueness of the world have continued to intrigue me throughout my life since I left the home of my biological family.

There are parallels and similarities between my leaving home during my eighteenth year and Abraham leaving his home at seventy-five. Indeed, I moved from a place where I felt comfortable, safe, and content to a place that was uncomfortable, risky, and threatening.

Abraham decided to leave his father's house and land in Haran and venture out into unknown territory heading toward what he understood from God to be the Promised Land. Now this was a man who lived among people who saw a god in every tree, gods behind every cloud, and a counsel of gods who met in the mountains to decide whether rain or drought would be the weather. How Abraham received direction from one God who became the God of the patriarchs is a mystery.

Abraham was seeking a place. Yet why he decided to go out into unknown territory following the leadership of this one God is a mystery. "Go from your country and your kindred and your father's house to the land that I will show you" was the instruction

Abraham heard. If you were convinced that such a voice were speaking to you with such a bizarre invitation, how would you respond? Perhaps at times the speaking would be only a faint whisper, while at other times it would sound with alarming clarity. You might be able to shake it off or ignore it but following the voice would be hard. Wouldn't this have been even more difficult in Abraham's day? To leave the house and land of his father, Terah, must have been an agonizing struggle. He was not living in our twenty-first-century mobile society where people are expected to grow up and leave their parents, start new families in new places, and keep in touch daily by e-mail.

The how and why of Abraham's decision remain mysteries to us. A summary statement of Abraham's is "Then he moved on from place to place, going toward the southern part of Canaan" (Gen. 12:9). Abraham and his family became nomads, tent dwellers—people who would put up their tents one day and take them down the next. After Abraham started listening to God, he never again knew a settled life.

This is characteristic of the seeker's life. Abraham searched for a place, found a place, settled for a season, only to uproot and seek another place. Seeking a place became a life-long journey for Abraham. So it is for each of us. Have you ever had the notion that some day your life would be settled? I have, but I am finally permitting that illusive dream to die. When I was in high school, I was eager for college. That would be real life. In college I was eager to get on to seminary and make preparation for my vocation. I was eager to finish seminary so I could get on with real ministry. Having been a pastor for more than thirty years, I have not found life to be settled by any means. There always is another sermon to prepare, one more hospital visit to make, a funeral, a wedding, or one more phone call to make or receive. Then, through some unfairness and selfishness I was urged to leave a congregation and my life has been more unsettled than ever. Somewhere out there is the settled life, I continue fooling myself into believing.

Maybe all of us are nomads, pitching our tents first here and then there. We camp out at a committee meeting, a worship service, at our jobs, at school, drop by the house for a bite of food and a nap, and we're off again moving from place to place going toward the southern part of the Promised Land, wherever and whatever that is.

I suspect there were times when Abraham thought of his brother, Nahor, with envy. After all, Nahor was living a settled life in Haran, knowing he would die and be buried near their father. What a contrast Nahor and Abraham were. One lived a settled life with many gods, and one became a nomad following the direction of one God. Nahor and Abraham, two brothers, and which one is the household name?

Nahor's life was like an anchor. Abraham's life, after he got involved with God, was like a sailboat on the open sea. Nahor's life was lived in one house on one piece of land. Abraham was a tent dweller moving from place to place. I suspect many of us like Abraham's rewards and Nahor's lifestyle. However, the rewards of God for Abraham were not that clear at the time for him. The theme song for Abraham and his family must have been "On the Road Again." Neither Abraham nor his descendants considered the wandering a blessing. They didn't like the struggles and the changes and living in a state of having-not-yet-arrived any more than we do.

But what if the blessing wasn't the land at all? Maybe we've been missing the point all these years. What if the land was a metaphor for something more important than being able to call a piece of land your own and to build a house on it and keep a family there from generation to generation? What if the blessing was not the land but the relationship itself? The moment Abraham walked out of the house in Haran he began a journey that put him into a covenant-relationship with God. Centuries later when Moses died on the East Side of the Jordan looking over into Canaan, no bitterness or remorse is evident in his life. Maybe that was because the blessing was the relationship with God and not the land.

Relationships are for a lifetime. They change because life is constantly changing. Abraham's worldview changed because his covenant-relationship with God caused him to redefine his world. Abraham's life from the time he left Haran was much harder and much better than he ever imagined possible. Hasn't this been true of your relationship with God? Ever since you got involved with God hasn't your life been unsettled, moving from place to place, emotionally if not also geographically? The blessing is the relationship, and it contains both threat and promise. The threat is that we will be changed. The promise is that we will be changed. Ever since you got involved with God and left home, has your life gotten harder and better at the same time?

As we journey in relationship with God it becomes clearer that to live our lives on God's terms is to live a nomadic existence, moving from place to place. The only thing settled in our lives in the relationship with God is how unsettled our lives are. Relationships are for a lifetime and they are forever changing. The blessing from God is not the settled place but the relationship.

God said to the old man Abraham with no children, "I'm going to give you a dream so big it'll bust your seams. You'll never believe it. Come on, you craggy-faced old fellow, I'm going to give you a dream big enough, exciting enough, and challenging enough for a boy with peach fuzz on his face. You don't believe it? Well, just leave home and follow me."[2] And to everyone's surprise, maybe more to Abraham's surprise than anyone else's, he went.

There is no way that you and I can comprehend what that journey meant to a man or a woman in the time of Abraham and Sarah. When God said get up from where you are, leave the land you know, leave your clan and kin, as important as they were in that day, and go away to some place called Canaan and live in tents instead of this fine walled city—one of the most modern of ancient times—and go to some vague place, with some vague promise to a man his age of children to come, it was incredible that Abraham went. "Leave your old gods on the other side of the river," God said, "and all of the icons you've touched all your life; put your hand in my invisible hand, and I'm going to give you and all the world a wonderful dream."[3]

Would it seem a little extravagant to you if I should say that God has the same sort of dream for you? Would you believe me if I should say that this whole issue of being seekers is about God inviting us to leave the conventional wisdom of our generation, to believe there is more than just "making it big" for ourselves or even our families? To leave behind some of the things we've been taught by a culture that does not know where it's going and has become confused between dreams and nightmares? To walk toward a promise, reaching our hands out toward something we have not seen and may not see in our lifetimes? And to believe that God will not only bless us and our families by doing so but, believe it or not, that through us all the families of the earth may touch a blessing?

I never thought about all of this when I left home, a settled place of comfort, and began to move from place to place in life. Probably you have not thought of it either. But the value of reflection is the discovery of some of the possibilities and probabilities that lie before us when we seek a place, take the leap of faith to leave one place, and move to a new place that will become home for awhile. Indeed, seeking a place involves an enormous amount of time and energy. Each place we seek calls for a leap of faith. The seeking and finding a place strengthens the seeker's faith for the next leap.

In the process we discover that we are, as Glenn Hinson wrote, *Seekers After a Mature Faith.* The Promised Land is not about geography but about relationships, relationships with God and with fellow human beings, a place to be. Consciously and unconsciously we are searching for the relationships. Abraham and Sarah serve as the father and mother of all seekers. The relationship is the place we are seeking. As relationships evolve, change, grow, and deepen, so do we. Indeed, we are seekers, and the place we seek is a relationship with God and with each other.

QUESTIONS TO PONDER

1. When did your seeking a place begin?

2. What event prompted the beginning of your seeking?

3. What feelings are stirred up for you as you seek a place?

4. Compare and contrast your seeking a place with the seeking of Abraham and Sarah.

5. What is your response to the idea that the Promised Land is about relationship rather than about geography?

6. What is frightening to you about seeking a place?

7. What is exciting to you about seeking a place?

8. How is the movement from place to place a leap of faith for you?

2

SEEKING BLESSING

GENESIS 25:19–34

IN AN ATTEMPT TO DEMONSTRATE a continuing line of faithfulness, it is characteristic of biblical characters to state clearly their worship of the God of the patriarchs. Their way of doing that is to say that they serve and worship the God of Abraham, Isaac, and Jacob. My interest in Esau was piqued as I reflected, "I wonder why Esau was left out of the list of the patriarchs." Why is he never mentioned in the listing of the patriarchs? You may recall that he was the twin brother of Jacob, but apparently he was considered to be of less importance than Jacob in the development of the Hebrew people.

This is an illustration of how the story of the Hebrew people was told and recorded long after the events had occurred. Since Esau did not figure in those events as significantly as did Jacob, events in Esau's life are not highlighted, very little is told, and many have concluded Esau was not as important as Jacob was.

I think there is much to learn from Esau. I explore Esau's life in the next few pages. Join me in this journey and discover with me some characteristics in Esau that parallel our lives. A basic issue for both Esau and Jacob was the desire for and need of their parents' blessing. They needed the acceptance of their parents. They, like we, pursued that need. My hunch is that the more the blessing eluded them, the more they sought it.

Naturally, the lives of Esau and Jacob coincide and events overlap. Much of what is said about one cannot be said without some reference to the other. However, I will strive to avoid repetition as much as possible in these two chapters that deal with the twins.

Perhaps you have some familiarity with the family history of Esau and Jacob. Abraham and Sarah were their grandparents. Isaac and Rebecca were their parents. Rebecca was the daughter of Bethuel and the sister of Laban from the area of Mesopotamia. Isaac was forty years old when he married Rebecca. Apparently, they were married for several years before children were born because the writers of Genesis said that because Rebecca had no children Isaac prayed for children. This phrase was used other places in the Bible when a couple had been married for an extended period of time and did not have children.

Rebecca became pregnant and gave birth to twins, Esau and Jacob. David Steele has captured this event in poetic verse that clearly is based on the biblical account. His words are expressive.

> Rebecca reported, that beginning in the seventh month,
> Those babies in her womb were hyperactive.
> All that pummeling, with hands and feet,
> Was downright uncomfortable.
> She wished they would wait more patiently in line.
> The midwife had a time sorting out all the arms and legs.
> When, at last, she pulled the hairy baby into life
> She found the sibling clutching at his heel,
> As if to pull him back.
> It was an omen.
>
> They have no trouble with names for the twins.
> The elder with all that auburn fuzz is Esau . . . "Hairy"

(Later he will go by "Red").
The younger is named Jacob . . . "The Heel."
We'll see that's quite appropriate.
The parents dote, as well they should.
Right off the bat Isaac is attracted to the elder.
He likes the scrappy little fellow,
Thinks that covering of baby hair is macho!
That boy will make a man!
But, Jacob . . .
Well, Isaac is glad Rebecca cottons to him.
He seems a mite puny . . . and effeminate.
Too bad his second child is not a girl.[1]

The twins grew up and Esau became the outdoors type. He enjoyed hunting wild game. Jacob was of a quieter nature who preferred staying at home. On one occasion when Esau returned from an unsuccessful hunting trip, Jacob had a pot of soup cooking. You know what an appetite you can work up if you have been exercising strenuously outside—hiking or working or hunting. You also know how good the aroma of anything cooking smells when the hunger pangs and the odors of food collide. Well, this is what happened to Esau. He was certain that he would not live if he had to wait to prepare something for himself or if he had to wait until his mother cooked a meal. He asked Jacob for a bowl of soup.

As is often the case, the one from whom something is being requested wonders what's in it for him. How often there is some type of trade agreement made between siblings. One wants something the other has. The one who has what is desired offers a trade. So it was in this situation with Esau and Jacob. Jacob had something Esau wanted and he saw an opportunity to get what he wanted, Esau's birthright.

The right of the firstborn son was a later development that was apparently read back into this story as it was told through the generations. As the biblical story is unfolding, Esau and Jacob represent only the second generation of the Hebrew people. The first mention of the birthright issue is when it is inserted into this story.

Apparently, Esau did not realize the value of what he had. He readily traded his right as the firstborn son for a bowl of soup. The writers said that was all he cared about his rights as the firstborn son. The rights of the firstborn son later developed into an inheritance of two-thirds of the father's estate. However, there is no indication in the Isaac and Esau-Jacob situation that that was the case. What was most important was the blessing of the father to the eldest son. This blessing carried with it great significance. On the surface we may brush that aside as insignificant, but just consider how important it has been in your life to have the approval of your parents. Think seriously about the parent's approval that you never could quite receive. That's what the blessing was. It was the approval of the father and the encouragement that went with that approval.

Another thing that Esau did not realize was that his birthright really was not his to give away. Oh, he could promise it to Jacob if he wanted, but really it was up to Isaac to give the blessing. On the other hand, maybe Esau did understand that and so could make such a promise to Jacob knowing that he, Esau, would get the bowl of soup he wanted immediately and later also receive the blessing from Isaac as the firstborn son.

From the very outset the storyteller has set up conflict in the story suggesting that rivalry between Esau and Jacob went all the way back to prenatal times. This is an example of seeing the development of a situation and then reading back into the events the outcome of the relationship, suggesting that the conflict was there prior to birth. There is a sense that the rivalry between Esau and Jacob was common sibling rivalry. However, an added ingredient was the favoritism shown to each of them by their parents. Isaac preferred Esau because of his outdoor interests and the wild game that he killed and provided for his father. Rebecca preferred Jacob because he stayed home.

At age forty, Esau got married. That was the same age his father was when he married. Perhaps that is coincidental, but often in family life, children follow the pattern of their parents in decisions about vocation, education, and marriage. Esau married two Hittite women. Polygamy was a common practice and the early parts of the Hebrew scripture do not condemn the practice nor suggest there was anything wrong with it. Monogamy was a later development in Hebrew culture. The storyteller said that Judith and Basemath made life miserable for Isaac and Rebecca, but did not say how they made life miserable. I do know that if parents do not approve of the mate their child chooses, the parents are miserable and there really is nothing the child or the mate can do to overcome that basic prejudice. Usually the sooner the child and mate realize this and go on making up their lives together, the happier their lives will be.

I suspect there is a sense in which each child feels she is the least favored by the parents. That is part of the development of self-esteem. When parents make clear, obvious choices that they prefer one child over another, the result is terribly destructive in the lives of both the chosen and the unchosen child. In the case of Esau and Jacob, each had a parent who favored him and yet each was emotionally in a position of striving always to gain the favor of the other parent. What a destructive family system that was. If your family is like that, you need to get professional help to work through those conflicts now.

The announcement came from Isaac to Esau that he was now ready to give him his blessing as the elder son. He wanted Esau to prepare him a meal and then he would give the blessing. No reason is given as to why Isaac wanted to eat before he gave the blessing to his son. In any case Esau headed for the woods and the hunt of wild game. Rebecca had heard Isaac's promise and so she interceded on behalf of Jacob by telling him how he could deceive his father.

It is significant in the story that Jacob never voiced concern about cheating his brother. His concern was that he would get caught in the act. How could he pretend to be Esau and Isaac not recognize him? Esau had a very hairy body. Jacob knew that touch and embrace would be part of the blessing. Rebecca suggested that Isaac was not so perceptive. She indicated that he wouldn't know the difference between venison and goat and that Jacob could wear Esau's clothes and cover his arms with goatskins and Isaac would never know the difference. With the encouragement of his mother, Jacob was convinced he could pull off this charade.

In many ways it is surprising that Isaac could have been fooled so easily. Surely Isaac could tell the difference between human hair and goat hair. Although he was blind or nearly so, he had other senses, but they rendered a split decision. It was a toss-up for Isaac. Two of the five senses told him that it was Jacob rather than Esau in front of him. The sound of Jacob's voice troubled Isaac but the hairy, goatskin covered arms and finally the smell of Esau's clothes settled Isaac's questions and he gave the blessing to Jacob.

Of course, when Esau returned he was enraged. He approached his father for a blessing but there was none left for him. We have difficulty understanding this. A mistake had been made. More seriously, a conscious, intentional action to deceive had taken place. So why did Isaac not just correct the mistake? It was all there on instant replay and Esau's voice immediately activated the instant replay button in Isaac's mind. It was to no avail. Part of the Eastern thinking, especially Hebrew thinking, was that to speak was to act and once a word was spoken it could not be retracted in any way. Thus the blessing stood. Listen to what Isaac said to Esau:

> "Behold, away from the fatness of the earth shall your dwelling be,
>   and away from the dew of heaven on high.
> By your sword you shall live, and you shall serve your brother;
>   But when you break loose you shall break his yoke from
>   his neck." (Genesis 27:3–40)

Apparently Esau was biding his time, expecting Isaac to die at any time. His plan was to have two funerals at once. When his father died he planned to kill Jacob. Rebecca perceived Esau's plan, sent for Jacob, and sent him away supposedly to find a wife, but the primary reason was to save him from the wrath of Esau.

Once again David Steele has captured this part of the story poetically.

Esau is furious
When he learns his brother has purloined the prize.
He'll not leap manfully across the net
To shake the victor's hand.
Esau is furious
With his conniving mother, his senile dad,
But most of all he's angry at himself
For being such a sucker.
So Jacob now is heir to mighty Abraham's legacy,
And he's expected to kow-tow to that mama's boy?
He nearly throttles Jacob then and there.

Let them gloat!
Esau knows he is no match for Jacob and Rebekah
In a battle of wits.
But it takes no Machiavellian mind
To know that Jacob will have trouble governing the clan
From a pine box.
The elder brother bides his time,
Watches his father weaken day by day,
And lets his mother know
In no uncertain terms:
"On the day dad dies
Get ready for two funerals."
Is he bluffing?
Rebekah thinks not.

Of course she has a plan
(She always does).

When she and Isaac are alone, she plays her ace.
"It's time that Jacob took a wife," she says,
"And I'll not have him mating with these local girls
As Esau has.
I'll have no further native cows
Mooning 'round my living room.
My son deserves a proper wife,
A girl of breeding, culture, and tradition
Who understands the greatness of our clan.
It's time you sent your son to Haran."
The old man acquiesces . . . . What can he do?
Secret plans are made for Jacob's trip.[2]

With Jacob out of the house and out of the setting, Esau begins to cool down from his rage. The rowdy one had been impulsive about trading a birthright for a bowl of soup. Eagerly he had gone to hunt, perhaps whenever the notion struck him. He had been ready to beat Jacob to a pulp. Eventually, he became calmer and more serene with Jacob out of sight and reach. Esau married again, this time to a member of the clan, Mahalath, who was the daughter of Ishmael. She was his first cousin. Apparently, Esau did not know until the blessing of Jacob that his parents had disapproved of his marriages to the two Hittite women. I wonder if he hoped and anticipated this marriage would make it up to them. Of course, it didn't. At least there is no indication that Esau was in any better favor with them, especially his mother, than he ever had been. Once people get an image set in their minds of what a person is like, it is so difficult to get them to change. Parents seem especially to suffer from this malady.

Now the story of Esau skips twenty years while the writers tell about events in Jacob's life. The next time Esau is mentioned is at the time Jacob is going to come face to face with him after twenty years of separation. Put yourself in Esau's place. How would you feel as you prepared to meet you brother after all of the conniving he had done? What would be your reaction as you prepared to meet him? Jacob certainly expected the worst, perhaps because he knew how he would have reacted if the situation had been reversed.

Jacob did everything he could think of to appease Esau. All of it was wasted on Esau. As soon as Esau saw Jacob, he ran to him, threw his arms around him and kissed him. (The description is so similar to Jesus' parable of the loving father. I wonder if this story was the background for Jesus telling that story.) This aspect about Esau is hidden, nearly lost, certainly forgotten by practically everyone who knows the story of Esau and Jacob. Jacob offered Esau all kinds of animals: goats, sheep, camels, and donkeys. Esau brushed all of that aside when he said, "I have enough, my brother; keep what you have" (Genesis 33:9). Do you know anyone who ever said, "I have enough"? We are more like John D. Rockefeller. When asked how much money is enough, Rockefeller replied instantly, "Just a little bit more." Jacob continued to insist until Esau finally accepted the gifts. I get the impression in reading this part of the story that Esau's reception of the gifts was the only way Jacob could have his guilt assuaged. Esau's warm, loving, forgiving acceptance of Jacob was more than Jacob could handle. He had offered the gifts to win Esau's favor, but that had not been necessary. Then Jacob was at a loss. He felt so vulnerable, so indebted to Esau, so much at his mercy. It seemed even more necessary for Jacob to make things equal and even.

Esau then volunteered to travel with Jacob to Edom, but Jacob insisted that Esau go ahead. Esau offered to leave some of his men to journey with Jacob, but again Jacob refused. How uncomfortable Jacob was with forgiveness and acceptance. How comfortable Esau was. Obviously, he had worked through his bitterness, resentment, and rage at Jacob during their twenty-year separation. Now he was able, willing, eager to be in Jacob's company, but it was more than Jacob could handle. Jacob never did make it to Edom. He and Esau never were really together, although this event of meeting and reconciliation occurred.

Later on when Isaac died Esau and Jacob met again at the funeral to bury their father. Isaac died at the age of 180 according to the biblical account. He had lived about eighty years since the rift between Esau and Jacob. What if Esau had stayed with his plan to wait around until his father died and then kill Jacob? Consider how long he would have had to keep his resentment alive. Eighty years. People do it all the time, but it is so destructive and it controls and colors everything else they do. Anger is a natural response for anyone to make who has been mistreated, cheated, and betrayed. It is not unusual for the anger to sour and become resentment. But the person who is resentful must make a decision whether to hang on to the resentment or to give it up. We do have control over how long we are going to resent another person.

Sometime during the twenty years of separation Esau decided he had resented Jacob long enough and he gave it up. Thus when he saw Jacob again he was not encumbered by unfinished business. I don't know about you, but I had not discovered this characteristic in Esau until I began researching for this chapter. I knew he was the forgotten twin, having been left out of the list of patriarchs, and I began by asking, "I wonder how Esau felt?" There is some slight reconciliation in the biblical account because as the writers recorded the death and burial of Isaac they said that his sons Esau and Jacob buried him. There Esau was restored to the position of being the elder son.

There is evidence in the biblical record that early on in life Esau was a rowdy type of person who was perhaps not as easy to manage as Jacob was. At least in the early years Jacob was more dutiful while Esau was more independent. Esau did have characteristics that were liabilities. He seemed to live only in the immediate moment and to live by the light of only what was obvious. He did not see the value of being the family's representative to others and for the next generation.

Assets of Esau include his physical vigor and his warm-hearted, magnanimous spirit. When his father wanted food he was eager to take off on the hunt to provide the game. Much later, his forgiveness of Jacob made all of Jacob's gestures look small and like exactly what they were—bribes.

Esau responded naturally with anger to having been cheated and betrayed by his brother and his mother. Of course he contributed some to that situation and he may have had as much anger at himself as anyone and projected it onto them. In any case some way, somehow during the twenty-year interim, Esau dealt appropriately with his anger and resentment rather than letting them deal with him. He took control of those emotions rather than giving them permission to control him. The result is that this one who wanted and needed his father's blessing learned the art of forgiveness. Although he did not become known as one of the outstanding patriarchs of Israel, his life can serve as an illustration of the value and worth of learning the art of forgiveness. Then Esau put into practice what he had learned in relationship with the very person who had been the source of so much pain, hurt, struggle, and anguish in his life. I recommend the life of Esau to you for your exploration and study that you might learn how and where your story and Esau's story intersect. Stop at that intersection and experience the blessing there.

QUESTIONS TO PONDER

1. What meaning does the birthright in Esau's story have for you?
2. What is the meaning of parental blessing in your life?
3. How has the desire/need for a parent's blessing contributed to your being a seeker?
4. How do you think Esau came to be able to forgive Jacob?
5. What significance is there in Esau's statement, "I have enough"?
6. What events have occurred in your life that are parallel to the events in Esau's life?
7. How does examining Esau's life contribute to understanding your life more clearly?

3

A TRICKY SEEKER

GENESIS 28:10–22

THE BIBLE IS A COLLECTION OF STORIES. The stories revolve around the lives of a clan of people and their involvement with God. They interpret their interaction with other clans that lived around them in light of their understanding of God. Long before any of the material currently contained in the Bible was written down, it was told over and over from generation to generation around the campfires of a clan known as the Israelites. The term *Israelites* identified the descendants of Israel, whose alias was Jacob, whose first and most descriptive alias was trickster. It is about and from this trickster seeker that we explore, examine, and learn in this chapter.

Jacob's story is one of the more fascinating ones in the Bible. Jacob was a rogue and a scoundrel, and yet, he is identified as one of the big three. Always he is listed with Abraham and Isaac but always the listing is about the God of Abraham, Isaac, and Jacob. (In light of the previous chapter I want to change the listing to read the God of Abraham, Isaac, Esau, and Jacob.) The listing by the biblical writers is significant. They are not holding up Abraham, Isaac, and Jacob as wonderful role models for us. They are pointing out that God sought to be the God of three very different, varied, and unusual characters. God was willing to be the God of Jacob but that did not mean everything Jacob did was sanctioned or justified by God. Nor does it suggest that Jacob was in any way seeking God other than to use God for his advantage and purposes, as we shall see. What it means is that God will receive all who offer themselves to God and will strive to make something out of them even when they continue to make a mess of life themselves. What an apt description of Jacob!

The record of Jacob's life begins in Genesis 25:21, and it is one of the oldest recorded tragic comedies. The editors of Jacob's story had a flare for the dramatic. Clues are given at the outset that problems will develop later in the story. First, the name Jacob is defined as meaning trickster. Like a red flag to the reader or listener, this meaning says, "Be on the lookout in Jacob's story for times when he tricked people." A second hint at trouble is when we are told that Isaac and Rebecca each favored a son. Favoritism caused problems, and Jacob paid a huge price for being doted on and indulged.

Jacob used manipulation and exploitation to trick people into giving him what he wanted. More accurately, Jacob tricked people into giving him what he was going to take from them anyway. Jacob's approach just caused people to feel better about being ripped off, until they realized what had happened to them.

Jacob's story, as later told by his descendants, reveals that often Jacob's way of dealing with a difficult situation was to con a person into giving him what he wanted and then look for an escape route. Jacob had the ability to enrage others. His name became synonymous with trickery.

The first trick Jacob pulled was trading a bowl of soup to his twin brother, Esau, for his right as the elder son. He caught Esau at a vulnerable moment. Con artists are especially skilled at that. Jacob had a huge pot of red bean soup cooking. The aroma would make your mouth water. It made Esau's mouth water when he got within smelling distance. Esau was hungry and the aroma convinced him he would starve to death before he could fix lunch.

(I've known a few teenagers in my day that responded the same way.) Esau asked Jacob to give him some soup. Jacob said, "Sure, but you know, don't you, that there is no such thing as a free lunch. The price for this bowl of soup is your rights as the firstborn son." Esau said, "Fine. If I don't get something to eat right now, I'll die of starvation and what good will firstborn rights do me if I'm dead!" I suspect Jacob had been plotting for a long time, looking for the time and place to put the squeeze on Esau to get the firstborn rights. As an aside, the rights of the firstborn developed much later in the Israelite clan but are read back into the plot of this story. That adds to the drama and intrigue of the story. Perhaps on another level, every person has some basic right that another person wants and will make a variety of offers to obtain.

With the help of his mother, Rebecca, Jacob played his second trick, this one on his father, Isaac. With this trick, Jacob's nature as a con artist is demonstrated more clearly. Isaac was convinced that his death was imminent. He thought he should give his final blessing to Esau, his older son. He sent Esau out for a McVenison burger, large fries, and a cola. Rebecca overheard the conversation, told Jacob about it, and suggested a masquerade to trick Isaac. Jacob was ready for any trick that would benefit him. His concern was not about deceiving his father or about stealing from his brother. His only concern was getting caught. Jacob was good enough at his charade to fool his dad, but he infuriated Esau.

Here is when Jacob the con artist became an escape artist. This was the first of several times that Jacob sought a spatial solution to a relational problem. He attempted to put as much space as possible between himself and Esau, thinking that would solve his problem. Jacob ran from the presence of Esau and sought refuge at Grandpa's house. Jacob may have been one of the first people to run to grandparents for protection, but he wasn't the last.

While Jacob was en route to his grandfather's house he had an experience that he described as an encounter with God. Many people like Jacob have found themselves in a tight spot because of their own doing, baptized their situation in religious language, and given their actions a ring of piety, which nevertheless has a hollow ring. Jacob, first, and then many of his kinfolk since, in the midst of a crisis, frightened for his life, sought to strike a bargain with God. Jacob had a dream of a stairway reaching from heaven to earth. When he awoke from his dream he concluded that he ought to make an agreement with God. Notice how the promise Jacob made is worded so that it is all to Jacob's benefit. "God, if you will be with me and protect me on the journey I am making and give me food and clothing, and if I return safely to my father's home, then you will be my God" (Genesis 28:20–21). What a favor Jacob is going to do for God! Jacob did what Augustine described later, "Good men use the world to enjoy God, whereas bad men use God to enjoy the world" (*De Doctrina Christiana* 22.20). David Steele poetically summarized this event at Bethel.

> *Jacob is a new man*
> *As he sets off on his adventure.*
> *The frightened, lonely boy is gone.*
> *He's got the Lord now.*
> *There's a spring in his step,*
> *A song in his heart,*
> *And peace in his soul.*
> *Haran, here he comes!*
> *So Jacob's known that happy day*
> *"Born again" is what we call it.*
> *But should you meet him on his way,*
> *Keep your hand upon your wallet!*[1]

Jacob continued on his way to Grandpa's place. There he met his first cousin, Rachel. As soon as Jacob saw Rachel, he ran up to her, kissed her, and began to cry. People react in a variety of ways when they meet the person of their dreams, but bursting into tears is not what I think of as the usual reaction. What a shock it must have been for Rachel to have this stranger come running across the desert, grab her in his arms, lay a huge kiss on her, and then begin to cry! The biblical writer says that Jacob cried for joy. Maybe that was some solace for Rachel. I think Jacob also cried from relief. He felt safe now that he had reached Grandpa's house and met a beautiful woman, for which he had not bargained. But now that he had met her, the bargaining would begin.

Rachel ran ahead and told her father about the guy she had kissed and made cry. Then Jacob met his uncle Laban, his mother's brother, and told him about the con job he had done on his father and brother and Laban responded, "Yes, indeed, you are my own flesh and blood" (Genesis 29:14). Was Laban referring to the con artist in Jacob that revealed his kinship to him? Do you hear the humor captured by the storytellers?

Laban and Jacob spent the next twenty years tricking and conning each other. First, Laban got Jacob to work seven years in order to marry Rachel. Then, Laban added trick to trick by giving Jacob Rachel's older sister Leah instead of Rachel and telling him it just was not right for his younger daughter to marry before the older one did. Here was a father who had his own rule about the older child. But Laban had a solution for Jacob. He suggested seven more years of work from Jacob for Rachel, and Jacob agreed. After fourteen years of work, Jacob had two wives, each wife had a handmaiden, and before many more years had passed Jacob had fathered sons by all four women, a total of twelve sons. When the twelfth son was born, Jacob decided it was time to take his clan and move on. When he made that decision Jacob seemed content to take his family and go until Laban suggested that Jacob deserved some payment for the prosperity which Jacob seemed to have brought him. Never one to pass up an opportunity to take something for nothing, Jacob suggested that Laban give him all the black lambs and the spotted goats. Laban agreed but before sundown he had his sons cull all the black sheep and spotted goats from the flock and move them a three-day's journey away from the flock. Laban had played his ace. The con artist Jacob had been conned again. One thing certain about a con artist, at least this one named Jacob, is that he was never without a trump card. Jacob's trump card was an unusual understanding of animal husbandry. Jacob believed that if the animals saw spotted branches when they were breeding their offspring would be spotted. Frankly, I have not a clue about the rationale for this understanding of animal husbandry. Nevertheless, Jacob got his servants to wave spotted branches in front of the strong, healthy animals when they were breeding. They were to make certain they did not hold the spotted branches in front of the weak animals when they were breeding. The result was that Jacob had the healthier, younger, stronger, and more numerous flock.

Apparently, Jacob and his clan remained with Laban for a considerable time after he had said it was time for them to go. They hung around long enough for the animals to breed, give birth, and for Laban's sons to discover that Jacob now had the bigger, stronger, better herd of animals. To state it mildly, they were outraged!

In the words of the song "The Gambler," popularized by Kenny Rogers, you have "to know when to hold 'em and know when to fold 'em." Jacob knew when to fold 'em. He heard Laban's sons' outrage and noticed that Laban was not nearly as friendly as he had been earlier. Jacob read the signs of the times and concluded it really was time to go back to his parents. He gave a religious interpretation to the decision, claiming he had a message from God that said, "Go back to the land of your fathers and to your relatives" (Genesis 31:3). He told this to Leah and Rachel as if he had had a dream about the production of a strong, healthy flock as sign from God that he was to leave. When he told the story to Leah and Rachel, Jacob left out the part about cheating their father out of the healthier, younger, and stronger animals. Jacob was a trickster and a rogue, but he portrayed himself to his wives as a righteous, obedient servant of God. Jacob had painted himself into a corner. He was in a tight spot and once again the old escape artist came to the surface and he turned tail and ran.

It was three days before Laban knew that Jacob was gone. That is how a con artist operates. He is smooth in one's presence, but when he is gone, anger mounts as people discover they have been had. Laban got a posse together and caught up with Jacob at Gilead. There was no balm in Gilead that day! Jacob and Laban argued and argued. Finally, they made a truce. They drew a covenant that stated, "The Lord watch between you and me, when we are absent from one another." Some suggest this is a sanctified farewell, but it is not. It is a clause in a rogue's bargain requesting that the all-seeing God keep matters straight between two people who cannot and will not trust each other. No doubt Jacob was glad to escape from Laban alive. David Steele's poetry once again is descriptive.

> *So once again, our hero gets*
> *To leave a place midst angry threats.*
> *My Jacob surely has the knack*
> *Of causing folks to blow their stacks!*[2]

The escapist strategy has two glaring weaknesses. The strategy is neither lasting nor practical. Usually when one escapes he takes the germ of the problem with him into the new situation and before long the same set of circumstances is reproduced all over again. Additionally, when the pressure increases to the point that escaping from something is a person's only concern, often the person flees into something worse than that from which he was seeking escape.

Amos spoke of fleeing a lion, only to run into a bear (Amos 5:19). This describes Jacob. He fled his brother and ran into Laban, got into the same kind of trouble and concluded he would be much better off back with his parents and headed that direction. Only while he was on the run back toward home did he suddenly remember that in addition to Isaac and Rebecca being there, Esau would be there too, the very one from whom he had sought escape the first time. Then someone brought Jacob word that

Esau was on his way with four hundred men to meet Jacob. It was nearly enough to make him tremble.

Reality is whatever a person is up against. Jacob the escapist came of age at this point. He at least acknowledged that he was up against the reality of facing his brother. He recognized that he could run but he could not hide.

Jacob finally learned something from his past: the only way out is the way through. Jacob was out of time and out of space. He had to face Esau. Good news comes in facing up to the bad news rather than running from it. Jacob adopted a new strategy mainly because he had to, but at least he changed his pattern of dealing with the mess he had made. I suspect we are a lot like Jacob at this point. Who of us ever changes just for the sake of changing? Many of the changes we make in our lives are out of the necessity rather than just a desire or decision to change.

The night before meeting Esau Jacob spent beside the Jabbok River, dreaming and wrestling with a messenger. Who was the messenger? The messenger had many faces. Jacob was wrestling with Esau whom he had cheated. He was wrestling with his father to whom he had lied. He was wrestling with the dark side of himself whom he was afraid to see in the light of day. He was wrestling with God who was calling him to accountability for his actions. It was a time of reckoning in Jacob's life. Through the struggle Jacob seemed finally to learn that the way out is the way through, not around, over, under, or behind. Jacob demonstrated that he was capable of learning from life and becoming different in the future because of the past. David Steele has a verse that summarizes this portion of Jacob's life.

> So Jacob, master wheeler dealer
> Is Israel, the wounded healer.
> And we among the human throng
> Are called to come and limp along.[3]

Even with a change in strategy, much of the old manipulative, cunning approach was still in Jacob. He sent gifts ahead to

Esau. What was Jacob's reasoning? Jacob said, "I will win him over with the gifts, and when I meet him, perhaps he will forgive me" (Genesis 32:20). Then, he lined up his family in a processional with the ones he liked least in the front of the processional. He put the concubines and their children first, then Leah and her children and then Rachel and her son, Joseph, at the rear. Jacob hid behind the women and children. What a macho man!

Jacob went out to meet Esau and bowed seven times to him. I get the impression that every time he bowed Jacob was looking out of the corner of one eye at Esau and out of the corner of the other eye to see where the exit signs were. When Jacob and Esau finally met after twenty years, it was a great reunion but they didn't become fast friends or stay together very long. On meeting Esau, Jacob gave him a beautiful flower, saying, "To see your face is for me like seeing the face of God. . . ." Then he plucked off the bloom by adding, "Now that you have been so friendly to me" (Genesis 33:10). The old manipulative pattern was still at work.

Esau wanted them to travel together with him leading the way, but Jacob said the children were weak and the sheep and cattle had their young. Esau might move too fast and the whole herd would die. Jacob added, "I will follow slowly, going as fast as I can with the cattle and the children, until I catch up with you in Edom" (Genesis 33:14). Do you believe Jacob?

Esau wanted to leave some of his men with Jacob to help him since his children were weak and his flocks were young. Jacob would have none of that. Jacob batted down Esau's every offer of reconciliation. Jacob was really uncomfortable relating to Esau. It was as if Jacob projected onto Esau what he would feel had the situation been reversed. Receiving forgiveness seems to have been more than Jacob could handle. They parted and lived in separate places and as far as we know never were together again except at their dad's funeral. Of the two, Jacob has gotten the most ink in the Bible and the most comments through the centuries. But the evidence is that Esau came to terms with the way Jacob manipulated and exploited him, then was able to forgive Jacob and live without bitterness or resentment. Jacob never came to terms with Esau. It seems that Jacob did not want to relate to Esau. He was unwilling to take that risk. Jacob preferred to wrap up in himself, and that made for a very small package.

Jacob made some great strides in his life, but one area where he failed to learn from his past was in his parenting. The tendency is for parents to relate to their children just like their parents did or in just the opposite way. Jacob acted just like his parents. His parents had shown favoritism to their sons. Isaac favored Esau and Rebecca favored Jacob. While Jacob enjoyed all of the attention that his mother gave him, there was no way that she could compensate for what Jacob needed—the love, affection, and attention of his father. So he was eager to use Rebecca's plan to get his father's acceptance, blessing by hook or by crook.

In spite of all the pain that Jacob experienced from the flaw of parental favoritism, when it came time for him to be a father he made the same mistake. He caused the same kind of havoc among his children as his father and mother had evoked in him and Esau. Jacob favored Joseph, his youngest son and the son of his favorite wife, Rachel. The brothers got rid of Joseph and it nearly killed Jacob. What is even more tragic is that after Joseph was gone, Benjamin was born to Rachel and Jacob, and Jacob made the same tragic mistake. He repeated the pattern and favored Benjamin. H. G. Wells once observed that "the only thing we learn from history is that we do not learn from history." Certainly in the segment of his life as a parent to his children, this was true for Jacob.

What if Jacob were a member of your family? What if you were telling his story to your children? How would you tell the story? What about when you decided to write down the story so that it could be preserved and passed on to generations yet to be born? How would you edit the story? Would you have aired all of the family's dirty laundry for anyone to hear or read? Well, the biblical writers did. They were willing to run such a risk to tell the story of Jacob and our lives are richer for our having an unglossed version of his life. The unglossed version enables us to see ourselves in Jacob. We don't really like to admit that, but there we are. We can learn from Jacob, learn from his willingness to stop being an escapist and to discover that the way through is the only healthy way out. We also can learn from his failures. Jacob never did learn how destructive favoritism was in family life. Right before us on the pages of Jacob's story we can see the destructiveness of both resentment and favoritism. Read for yourself the last twenty-five chapters of Genesis and become very familiar with your spiritual ancestor, the trickster seeker named Jacob. The same God who sought to help and guide Jacob wants to help and guide you and me. If we will become familiar with Jacob, we will become even more familiar with ourselves and with how Jacob is a part of who we are. And we will discover that God is willing to take the lives we offer and work with us to shape our lives into lives of meaning and value and reflection of God's love for the world.

The phrase "the God of Abraham, Isaac, Esau, and Jacob" says more about God than it says about them. Clearly, the phrase suggests that God was willing to take them and make something out of them. If you will permit this God to become your God, this God will take you, who you are, what you offer to God, and make something out of you. If this God becomes your God, it says a lot more about God than it says about you. This God will become the God of Abraham, Isaac, Esau, Jacob, and you. What a motley band of seekers!

QUESTIONS TO PONDER
1. What troubles you about Jacob?
2. What intrigues you about Jacob?
3. In what ways is Jacob a seeker?
4. Where is God in Jacob's story?
5. What is the value of Jacob's story for us today?
6. Where and how does your story intersect with Jacob's story?

4

A Suffering Seeker

JOB 30:20–31

ONCE IN A WHILE a person comes along who deals with a situation or event in life in a way that forever alters the way many people look at similar events. That person's insight, experience, and understanding cause others to ask questions they would never have asked, to understand events and circumstances differently, and to alter perceptions. Job was such a person. The events and circumstances that happened in Job's life put Job on a path of seeking and searching. The events that happened to Job are unbelievable.

There are those who read the book of Job and conclude that all of those tragedies could not have happened to one person in such a short amount of time. This view interprets the character of Job as a composite person. The story is written in dramatic form to make a point about God. Job's story is a parable. The parable of Job raises two vital questions: why do people suffer, more specifically, why do righteous people suffer, and why are righteous people faithful to God? The text of Job wrestles throughout with these two questions.

Examine Job's experience with me. We will discover that in the midst of and through all the suffering he experienced, Job was a seeker. He was seeking meaning and purpose in life as well as the meaning of relating to God. This story will disclose some insights about God that Job discovered. These insights became part of the scenery and background for everyone after Job who has sought to know and relate to God.

Job's experience with suffering was a wilderness wandering through which no one had ever journeyed. Yet, to read about Job is to read parts of our own stories and to see parts of our wilderness wanderings. The term *wilderness* means untamed area; uncharted territory; wild place; deserted area; uncultivated thicket of trees, vines, and thorns; area where no one has gone previously. If by chance someone has traveled through the particular wilderness of suffering, no good map has been left for others to follow. Perhaps Job's experience can serve as a compass to point out the direction to travel through the wilderness of suffering.

The Book of Job is one of the best pieces of literature anywhere. It is a watershed work on the issues of suffering and unfairness. People have understood God and suffering and unfairness in a completely different light after Job's experience. The character Job is often referred to as a person of great patience. That is an erroneous conclusion. Job experienced an unbelievable amount of pain, suffering, and hardship in a relatively short period of time, but he did not accept those events and suffering without questions, anger, and struggle. Job was a person willing to say what he thought and felt. Job was willing to confront God with his hurt, anger, and bitterness. Job stood his ground with his friends and his wife, resisting their accusations and advice. He also stood his ground with God, not usually our view of how one is to interact with God but an approach portrayed, described, and supported many places in the Bible and especially in Job.

Truly, Job was a man of sorrows acquainted with grief. Job lost property. His children died. He was left with three self-righteous friends and an embittered wife. The suffering gradually wore down Job's most cherished beliefs. He wondered how God could be on his side. He was squatting in a heap of ashes, the ruins of his life. He was broken and in despair. Frankly, unfairness and suffering are no easier to deal with today than they were 2500 years ago for Job. That is why we resonate so clearly with Job.

In a day, a single day, Job was wiped out emotionally and nearly physically. The Sabeans ran off with his oxen and slaughtered his hired hands. Lightning struck his sheep barn and burned up the whole flock, not to mention the shepherds. The Chaldeans rustled his camels and made short work of the camel drivers. And a hurricane hit the house where his seven sons and three daughters were having a party with such devastating effect that there was not enough of them left in the wreckage to identify. And then Job came down with leprosy.[1] And that was only Monday. Job could hardly wait for Tuesday!

A crisis of faith brewed inside Job. No wonder! Was God unfair? Such a notion called into question everything Job believed, but how else could he explain what had happened? He looked around for other examples of unfairness and saw that evil people sometimes prospered—they were not punished, as he wanted to believe—while at the same time there were godly people who suffered. For Job, the facts simply did not add up.

The story of Job is so contemporary because the facts do not add up for us either. Job's strident message of life's unfairness seems peculiarly suited to our own pain-racked lives. Eventually, some form of suffering will touch our lives. In essence there are two categories of people in the world, those who have experienced suffering and those who are going to experience suffering. After an extensive tour of the United States, the well-known German pastor and theologian Helmut Thielicke was asked what he saw as the greatest defect among American Christians. He replied, "They have an inadequate view of suffering."

Simply plug contemporary illustrations into Job's arguments: starving children in the Third World; justice-seeking people imprisoned; people who die in their prime; people faithful to God who get cancer, experience horrible suffering, and die; loving parents who lose children to accidents and disease. Mafia dons and spoiled entertainers profit obscenely from flouting God's rules. Corporate executives are paid millions of dollars while millions of people are out of work. People in power use power to divide people against each other. There are random killings, embassies crumpled in rubble, millions who live quiet, happy lives and seem never to give God a thought. Far from fading away, Job's questions about this world's unfairness have only grown louder and shriller. We still expect a God of love and power to follow certain rules on earth. Why doesn't God?

Many have taken the advice of Job's wife, "Curse God and die." Some Jewish writers began with a strong faith in God but saw it vaporize in the gas furnaces of the Holocaust. Face to face with history's grossest unfairness, they concluded that God must not exist. Others agree life is unfair but conclude God can't do anything about it. Still others project unfairness into the future and conclude there will be a time when exacting justice will work itself out in the universe. There also are those who insist that the world is fair. This echoes Job's friends. Many insist there are hidden reasons and explanations for the agony and suffering that occurs. They suggest there is a plan. Some even conclude that we aren't supposed to know the answers and therefore should not be asking the questions. Here is some of the common, helpless, worthless advice that we are often given, usually by people who, for whatever reasons, have not encountered the deep, destructive unfairness that we may be encountering. "God is trying to teach you something." Well, what is God trying to teach? If God wants me to learn something, then God needs to be clearer with the message. "Just remember there are people a lot worse off than you." This is a rather arrogant coping statement. It is a bit like the prayer of the Pharisee in Jesus' story who said, "God, I thank you that I am not like that person over there who has life so much worse than I. I'm thankful I didn't have a stroke like he did." Other advice says, "Count your blessings. At least you are still alive."

But being grateful for life does not remove the pain, suffering, and struggle caused by unfairness. Finally, there is one other way to explain the world's unfairness. Job was driven to this conclusion, which is a one-sentence summary of the entire book: life is unfair! Job's friends tempted him to sin and they themselves sinned by blaming God for what had happened. In essence, Job's friends were saying that God had caused the terrible things that had happened to Job. The writer of Job states clearly that Job did not give in to committing blasphemy, which is to attribute evil to God. The writer says, "Job did not sin by blaming God" (Job 1:22).

If we can come to the awareness that life is unfair, we may find guidance and insight to help us cope with suffering. Alberta B. Szalita, in a lecture at the Columbia (New York) University Psychoanalytic Center, suggested that suffering that is accompanied by insight and gradual emancipation from narcissistic self-involvement leads to empathy that, in turn, contributes to the resolutions of grief. With that comes a compassionate attitude toward others and a new commitment to life. Native Americans expressed it this way: "Don't judge another person until you have walked a mile in his moccasins."

Those who survived the most horrific suffering imaginable observed how others coped. "We who lived in concentration camps can remember the men who walked through the huts comforting others, giving away their last piece of bread. They may have been few in number, but they offer sufficient proof that everything can be taken from a man but one thing: the last of the human freedoms—to choose one's attitude in any given set of circumstances, to choose one's own way."[2] One has but to recall Milton's blindness, Beethoven's deafness, and Coleridge's headaches to remember the grandeur humanity has often achieved in spite of difficulties.

Dostoevski, who spent several years in the lonely exile of Siberia before becoming a great novelist, said, "suffering is the sole origin of human consciousness." Suffering, unless we abjure it and retreat from it, causes us to sharpen our wits, discipline our talents, and develop our possibilities.[3]

Once we are able to arrive at the conclusion that life is unfair, we are able to stop looking for a cause. We can stop asking, "Why did this happen?" We can begin searching for a response. Now that this has happened to me, what am I going to do? Job's friends and his wife continued to be hung up in the causal mode. They kept looking for and offering suggestions for what they thought were causes of his condition. Obviously, they believed that if they could find the exact cause of Job's problems, his anger, bitterness, and questioning would cease. But that isn't true. A child gets leukemia. The parents ask, "Why?" The medical team takes plenty of time explaining how the body works, what the situation was that led to the child developing the disease. There you have it. The doctors have thoroughly explained the cause of leukemia in language the parents clearly understand and the parents respond, "Why?" Their "whys" continue to be raised because of the unfairness. Their "whys" verbalize their anger. And there is no answer to the "whys." One helpful solution is to recognize what Job recognized: "Life is unfair."

Neither the biblical material in general nor the book of Job in particular ever explains the cause of pain and suffering. People are guided away from the issue of cause. They are pointed toward the issue of response.

Philip Yancey tells about a conversation he had with a friend who had had many unfair things happen to him, and who is in Yancey's opinion a kind of modern-day Job. Yancey asked him what he had learned that might help someone else going through a difficult time.

"To tell you the truth," Douglas said, "I didn't feel any disappointment with God.

"The reason is this. I learned, first through my wife's illness and then especially through the accident, not to confuse God with life. I'm no stoic. I am as upset about what happened to me as anyone could be. I feel free to curse the unfairness of life and to vent all my grief and anger. But I believe God feels the same way about the accident—grieved and angry. I don't blame him for what happened.

"I have learned to see beyond the physical reality in this world to the spiritual reality. We tend to think, 'Life should be fair because God is fair.' But God is not life. And if I confuse God with the physical reality of life—expecting constant good health, for example—then I set myself up for a crashing disappointment.

"God's existence, even his love for me, does not depend on my good health. Frankly, I've had more time and opportunity to work on my relationship with God during my impairment than before."

Douglas concluded, "If we develop a relationship with God apart from our life circumstances, then we may be able to hang on when the physical reality breaks down. We can learn to trust God despite all the unfairness of life. Isn't this really the main point of Job?"[4]

In the Sinai wilderness, God's guarantees of physical success—health, prosperity, and military victory—did nothing to help the Israelites' spiritual performance. And most heroes of the Hebrew scripture (such as Abraham, Joseph, David, Elijah, Jeremiah, and Daniel) went through trials much like Job's. For each of them, at times, the physical reality surely seemed to present God as the enemy. But each managed to hold on to a trust in God despite the hardships. In doing so, their faith moved from a "contract faith"—I'll follow God if God treats me well—to a relationship that could transcend any hardship.

Life is not fair, but God is. God is not life. Job's faith in God remained and that sustained him through the awareness, discovery, and acknowledgment that life is not fair.

Philip Yancey notes,

> . . . Despite the fact that all but a few pages of Job deal with the problem of pain, I am coming to the conclusion that Job is not really about the problem of pain.

Suffering contributes the ingredients of the story, not its central theme. Just as a cake is not about eggs, flour, milk, and shortening, but uses those ingredients in the process of creating a cake, Job is not "about" suffering; it merely uses such ingredients in its larger story, which concerns even more important questions, cosmic questions. Seen as a whole, Job is primarily about faith in its starkest form.[5]

A flash of light from a beacon on shore and then a long, dreadful time of silence and darkness—that is the pattern I find not only in the book of Job, but throughout the Bible. Recall tottery old Abraham as he neared the century mark, holding feebly to the lustrous vision that he would father a great nation. For twenty-five years that vision had seemed a desert mirage until one son, just one, was born. And as Abraham understood God communicating with him, he thought he heard God say, "Take your son, your only son, Isaac, whom you love and sacrifice him as a burnt offering."

Then there was Joseph, who heard from God in his dreams but landed at the bottom of a well and later in an Egyptian dungeon for trying to follow that guidance. And Moses, handpicked liberator of the Hebrew people, who hid in the desert for forty years, hunted by a pharaoh's security guards. And the fugitive David, anointed king on God's command, who spent the next decade dodging spears and sleeping in caves.

The baffling, Morse-code pattern of divine guidance—a clear message followed by a long, silent gap—is spelled out bluntly in 2 Chronicles (chapter 22 ff.). There the account is given of a rare good king, Hezekiah, who so pleased God that he was granted an unprecedented fifteen-year extension to his life. What happened next? "God left him to himself, in order to try him and to know all that was in his heart" (2 Chronicles 32:31).

Basically, the pattern shown in the stories of Job and other biblical characters who struggle with suffering is that pain is caused by suffering, there is a search for the cause, and then the sufferer gives a response. To get the full impact, search the speeches in the book of Job, looking for Job's own words. With all that happened to Job, we might expect to find him complaining about his horrible luck and miserable health and lamenting the loss of his children and fortune; but surprisingly, Job had relatively little to say about those matters. He focused instead on the single theme of God's absence. What hurt Job most was the sense of crying out in desperation and getting no response. That same feeling is described by many suffering people, perhaps best stated by C. S. Lewis, who wrote these words in the midst of deep grief after his wife's death from cancer:

> Meanwhile, where is God? This is one of the most disquieting symptoms. When you are happy, so happy that you have no sense of needing Him . . . you will be—or so it feels—welcomed with open arms. But to Him when your need is desperate, when all other help is vain, and what do you find? A door slammed in your face, and a sound of bolting and double bolting on the inside. After that, silence. You may as well turn away. The longer you wait, the more emphatic the silence will become.[6]

Suffering seems to involve two main issues: 1) who causes my discomfort and 2) my response. Most of us expend our energy trying to figure out the cause of our pain before we'll decide how to respond. Joni Eareckson Tada consumed two years exploring possible causes of the diving accident that left her a quadriplegic. But, as Joni found, to the extent that we concentrate on cause, we may well end up embittered against God.

In Job, the portion of the Bible that most vividly poses the question "Who causes pain?" God deliberately sidesteps the issue. God never explained the cause to Job. All the way through, the Bible steers from the issue of cause to the issue of response. Pain and suffering have happened—now what will you do? The great discussers of cause, Job's three friends, are dismissed with a scowl. The Bible is so clear on this point that I must conclude the real issue before Christians is not "Is God responsible?" but "How should I react now that this terrible thing has happened?" By no means can we infer that our own trials are specially arranged by God to settle some decisive issue in the universe. But we can safely assume that our limited range of vision will in similar fashion distort reality. Pain narrows vision. The most private of sensations, it forces us to think of ourselves and little else.[7]

In the wake of the tragedy that beset Job, three friends came to visit Job and supposedly to console him. But their real interest was an intellectual one. They wanted to understand all of this and know why all these things happened to Job. They turned the tragedies into a riddle to be resolved by reasoning and went to great lengths analyzing and speculating and theorizing about it. Job was not at all satisfied with the explanations his friends offered, but by this time he also was caught up in the game of seeking an explanation. He pursues that until he crashes right into the presence of God and demands an explanation from God.

Frederick Buechner points out that God did not comply with Job's demand for the simple reason that God could not. Job's capacities to understand were simply unequal to the immensities in question. "Explaining things fully to Job," says Buechner, "would have been like trying to explain Newtonian physics to a small-neck crab." The capacity of the one is simply not equal to the immensity of the other. So, nowhere in the Book of Job is there an attempt to explain things fully to this suffering man.[8]

Explanations were not really what Job needed most in that time of tragedy. How could he go on living with all those empty chairs at the breakfast table? That was the burning issue for Job, as it is for every person in the wake of tragedy. What am I going to do with what is left—this world of mine that now is so different and so much less than what I used to have? Think back to a tragedy that interrupted your life. If there had been a chart on the wall that explained exactly how all the events of the tragedy came about, would you have been satisfied? Of course not, because tragedy is more than a puzzling game to piece together. Tragedy, unfairness, suffering are awesome events to be lived through and coped with. The gift of hope is far more important in the midst of tragedy and suffering than the gift of understanding.[9] Where do we find this gift of hope? Job discovered that it grows out of a wrestling, questioning, and struggling with God that helps one arrive at a vision of who God is and what God does. God is the One who can take seemingly dead situations, make something out of them, bring them to life, and give them a future.

The eleventh chapter of Hebrews in Christian scripture refers briefly to well-known faithful seekers of God. This passage calls to the reader's mind Abraham, Sarah, Noah, and others, encouraging the reader to identify with and learn from these biblical characters. Some have labeled this chapter "the Faith Hall of Fame." I prefer to call that chapter "Survivors of the Fog," for many of the heroes listed have one common experience: a dread time of struggle like Job's, a time when the fog descends and everything goes blank. Torture, jeers, floggings, chains, stonings, sawings in two—Hebrews records in grim detail the trials that may befall faithful people.

Saints become saints by somehow hanging on to the stubborn conviction that things are not as they appear, and that the unseen world is as solid and trustworthy as the visible world around them. God deserves trust, even when it looks like the world is caving in.[10]

Life is unfair. God is fair. If we can cling to both of these convictions—life is unfair, God is fair—we can make it through any wilderness. And it is important to make it through because the way out really is the way through. Job concluded that life is not fair. What a wilderness that was! Job's conviction that God was fair gave him the courage, the hope, the faith to journey through the wilderness of unfair life. Through the journey he discovered for himself and for all of us who have lived after Job that life is unfair, God is fair, and the way out of the unfairness is the way through the unfairness with faith in a God who is fair.

What a gift the suffering seeker Job gave to all of us who have come after him. Many continue to view the experiences of suffering as coming from God as punishment or to teach them lessons or any number of other ancient views of cause-and-effect relationship. Job's struggle and approach, however, gives us a fellow seeker who was willing to express a different, healthier, more helpful approach. Thanks, Job. And thanks be to God for working through Job to help us discover that often life is unfair but God is always fair.

QUESTIONS TO PONDER

1. What do you think is the purpose of the book of Job?
2. Do you think Job is a historical figure or a composite character?
3. Does it matter which Job is?
4. What about Job's journey helps you in your journey?
5. What event has been the major source of suffering in your life?
6. What has been your experience/encounter with God in the midst of your suffering?

5

A REJECTED SEEKER

JOHN 4:5–42

I WONDER IF THERE IS ANYONE who is not seeking, searching in life. We may not know for what we are longing, but when we're still and quiet for a moment we can hear and feel the gnawing longing deep inside our beings. We may be in between adventures or disasters. One phase of life may have come to an end, but the new phase has not yet begun. I observe this during the commencement season each year. Commencement symbolizes all of the tension between "has been" and "not yet." I do not know what form your searching is taking right now. Maybe you're looking for a different job, hoping for a promotion, or anticipating retirement. Perhaps you feel lonely and want to develop some new friendships or closer relationships. Whatever your particular circumstances may be, you are a seeker, seeking meaning, purpose, happiness in life. Can they be found? How will you know when you have found them? What do you hope to get out of life? Is it all just a lost cause? When we feel helpless are we also hopeless?

St. Jude's Hospital is best known for its care of children with leukemia. St. Jude is the patron saint of hopeless cases and thus the name for the hospital. How St. Jude Thaddeus, one of Jesus' followers, got tagged as the patron saint of hopeless cases is unclear. He is called Jude by Luke and Thaddeus by Mark and Matthew, and he is traditionally credited with being the author of the short Epistle of Jude. Tradition claims that he preached in Mesopotamia and was put to death in what is now Iran. He seems to have been a faithful disciple, but somehow he became known as the patron of hopeless cases, and many people today have a devotion to him.

Today, we face seemingly "hopeless cases": the nuclear paste is out of the tube. Every time it seems to be under control, it oozes in another nation. Devastating diseases appear faster than cures, addiction is rampant, poverty is spreading, population is out of control, greed and selfishness are pervasive, and morality is skidding.

Harry Emerson Fosdick told the story of the young boy whose teacher asked: "Johnny, what shape is the world?" "I don't know," Johnny answered, "but my dad says it is in the worst shape it ever has been." On the days when we feel helpless and hopeless we agree that the world "is in the worst shape it ever has been."

If there ever was a lost cause, a hopeless case, it seems to me the Samaritan woman in John's Gospel represents lost causes and hopeless cases. Although we know very little about her, the profile that John provides for us reveals that she was a person who had been seeking, searching for happiness. For whatever reasons she had not experienced much meaning or satisfaction in life. The impression I have of her is that she had concluded life was not going to get any better for her and she was resigned to the mundane of routine. John's profile does not portray a person brimming with hope, but gives an impression of despair.

The first hint of despair is that she came to draw water at noon, in the heat of the day. Getting water out of a well that was a hundred feet deep was not child's play. Carrying a goatskin full of water from the well back into town was no light task, certainly in the desert heat of the Middle East. The usual time for going to the well for water was in the cool of the morning or the evening. So why was this woman making it so hard on herself?

She probably went to the well in the heat of the day for emotional protection. She could take the physical strain of the heat better than the strain caused by the emotional heat of other women's attitudes and actions. John subtly portrays this woman as an outcast. As the story unfolds, we are given hints as to why others shunned her.

Have there been times when you just wanted to avoid certain people because you felt condemned by them? You knew you couldn't measure up to their expectations or you knew they really didn't like you and you just didn't have the energy to be in the same room with them. I've been there! I've known people who felt I had nothing to offer. When my energy level is depleted, I'm just not up to being around people like that. I'm an outcast, as far as they are concerned, and I don't want to expose myself to the possibility of further expressions of dislike and disgust.

Any experience like this brings life up for review for us. We wonder about our worth. We also wonder if life holds any contentment and happiness for us. We go in search of meaning, value, and happiness, often unaware that we are searching and seeking. The distinct impression I draw from John's account of the Samaritan woman is that she had been beaten down and rejected so many times that she wasn't even aware she was seeking and desiring meaning and happiness in life.

Perhaps every avenue she had pursued toward happiness had led to a dead end. We learn she had been married five times. We don't know if each of her husbands died and she decided never to marry again because every time she did, her husband died. Or had more than one of them divorced her? In her culture all a man had to do was to declare publicly three times, "I divorce you," and it was done. Did she conclude it would be better just to live with someone? Was she just frightened of commitment and had been unable to stay in a marriage for very long? Or were her relational skills so poor that she couldn't make anything out of a relationship? What about the men she had married? Did they just see her as property or an object to be used and when she didn't do what they wanted, they simply got rid of her? I suspect she started every relationship with the dream that this one was going to provide her the protection and security she needed. She probably had given up any dreams of happiness, at least at the conscious level.

We've all done similar things and taken similar approaches toward our circumstances. We have concluded that happiness is out there somewhere. We have seen the solution as geographical or spatial or relational. If we can just move to a new house or a new city, all our problems will be over. If we can just get a little space and distance from the boss or the family or this neighborhood or this congregation, we'll be happy. If we can just find someone who understands us, our troubles will be over.

Will Rogers said that now and then he grew tired of the same old surroundings. Then he would wish for a new place to live and work. He said he would pick some city that sounded attractive. Before he moved, however, he would subscribe to the leading newspaper in his proposed new town and read that newspaper for thirty days. Rogers declared that he would always decide not to move. The news from where he planned to live was no better than the news where he was. Will Rogers was right. Happiness rarely comes from a change of locations, or a change of mates, or a change of situations of any kind. But many people go through life looking for happiness in all the wrong places.

Consider this woman at the well. Five times she had walked down the aisle to be married. Now she was living with a man to whom she was not married. Is that the kind of life she would have chosen for herself? It's doubtful. Was she looking in all the wrong places? Had events and circumstances over which she had no control merely devastated her options? Whatever searching and seeking she had been doing, conscious or unconscious, seems to have borne bad fruit.

When the woman arrived at the well, Jesus was there, having sent his disciples on into town to get some food. Apparently, Jesus was beginning to have some influence on his disciples, because before they met him, they, being Jews, would never have considered buying food from Samaritans. They would have considered it contaminated, unclean, and eating it would make them unclean before God. Perhaps they still thought that way and were looking for a kosher shop in the village.

Although the conversation between this woman and Jesus is the longest recorded conversation in the Bible Jesus had with anybody, there must have been more said than what John wrote. What John recorded is more like the summary notes of a committee meeting than a verbatim of what was said. Did the woman go ahead and approach the well when she saw a man was there? Did she and Jesus nod to each other or make sure their eyes did not meet? Rabbis did not speak to women in public, even to their wives and daughters. Did Jesus begin by saying good day to this woman? Did he ask, "How are you?" or comment, "It sure is hot, isn't it?" Surely the first thing Jesus said to this woman was not, "Give me a drink of water." Whatever preceded Jesus asking for a drink of water, the woman basically said, "Get it yourself." Her words were, "You are a Jew, and I am a Samaritan—so how can you ask me for a drink?" (John. 4:9) She knew the Jewish dietary and cleanliness rules. She knew Jesus knew them too. What perplexed her was Jesus' freedom to override the rules for a person and a relationship. Rules were made for people; people were not made for rules. Often rules are clung to long after their usefulness has passed.

One of my favorite stories is about the woman who always cut off one end of a roast before she cooked it. When her husband asked her why she did that, she said because her mother always did. In a short time they were with her mother and the man asked his mother-in-law if she still cut the end off a roast before she cooked it. She said she had done that all of her life. When he asked why, she said because her mother did. Now, it so happened that her mother was still alive and the man was able to ask his grandmother-in-law if she cut off the end of a roast before she cooked it. She confirmed that she did. He asked her why and she said because the pan was too small and it was only way she could get the roast to fit in the pan. Her daughter and granddaughter had clung to a valuable and worthwhile practice long after its usefulness had passed.

How did the woman know that Jesus was a Jew? Did his accent give him away? Was he wearing a phylactery, a leather container of Scriptures, which many Jewish men wore? Did Jewish men dress differently than Samaritan men, and she thus knew with just one look?

The woman was operating from the old standards and customs. Jews and Samaritans despised each other and never used the same utensils. Jews would never eat or drink from any dish that a Samaritan had touched. Men and women did not speak to each other in public. And it had been this woman's experience that no one, man or woman, treated her with anything but hate and disgust. But here was a man who was striking up a conversation with her. What did it mean? Why was he doing this?

Then Jesus offered her some living water and she said, "Mister, what kind of fool do you take me to be? You don't even have a bucket and this is a deep well. Not only that, this is Jacob's well. If it weren't for him, we wouldn't have this water. Now you aren't claiming to be greater than Jacob, are you?"

Notice what a literalist the woman was being. The well water was stationary. Jesus was talking about flowing water that the Jews identified as living water. It was a metaphor that was often used to refer to relationship with God. God was the source or the spring of water that quenched people's thirst to know God. To drink of that water did not mean a person never needed another drink; it just meant she didn't have to keep searching for the source. Many years ago when my great-great-grandfather decided to settle in Wayne County, Kentucky, he went to the head of the stream that flowed down into the valley. He discovered a fresh water spring at the head of the stream and at the foot of the mountain and there he built his house. He had to go to the spring every day to get water, but he didn't have to search for the source of clean, fresh water every day.

Jesus was seeking to point the Samaritan woman to the source of the spring of living water that really could quench her thirst for meaning, value, and happiness. Once the woman got over her wooden, literal interpretation and expectation of what Jesus was saying, she was eager to receive the water he offered because she had been thirsty for longer than she could remember. To this point in her life every drink she had taken had only made her thirstier.

Jesus urged her to get her husband and come back. The living water he offered was for all. The woman said she didn't have a husband. Again, as is John's writing style, Jesus knows more about people than has been revealed in the text. How Jesus knew the woman had been married five times and was living with a man but not married at the time is not disclosed. Notice that Jesus made an observation but did not condemn the woman or pass judgment on her. He simply said to her, "You have told me the truth" (John 4:18). It is amazing what acceptance will do to people and for people. Jesus may have been the first person this woman had met who related to her and responded to her on the basis of who she was. Jesus treated her with dignity and respect.

How did the woman respond? She told him the truth and concluded that he must be a prophet. Then, when she defended her tradition of worship, Jesus didn't debate with her. He simply declared that worship of God is not determined by geography but is defined by God's nature that crosses over every barrier: sexual identity, skin pigmentation, place, tradition, and liturgy. In the woman's mind, a God whose nature embraces all people in all places is a Messiah.

What did the woman do? She ran back into town, not with the answer, but only with the question, "Come and see the man who told me everything I ever did. Can he be the Messiah?" (John 4:29). The woman is a witness, but not a likely witness and not even a thorough witness. "A man who told me all that I ever did" is not the Apostles' Creed. "This cannot be the Christ, can it?" is not a convincing statement. But her witness is enough. It is invitational, not judgmental.

It is honest with its own uncertainty. Her witness doesn't hawk someone else's conclusions. She doesn't give packaged answers to unasked questions. Nor does she give thinly veiled ultimatums and threats of hell and assumptions of certainty on theological matters. She conveys her willingness to let her hearers arrive at their own affirmations about Jesus.

Buried deep within the earth lie vast deposits of diamonds, the world's most precious gem. Although these stones are tremendously valuable, until they are mined they remain useless—glimmering pebbles hidden beneath the surface. Some day these jewels will be unearthed and the world will marvel at their brilliance. One of the world's most famous diamonds is not white but rather a radiant blue. This diamond is cherished not only for its size and beauty, but also for its uncanny ability to conduct electricity—to energize those objects with which it comes into contact. The jewel is none other than the Hope diamond, the only one of its kind in the world.

Jesus is like the Hope diamond. He energized the woman at the well. Being in his presence conducted a power of hope to her that uplifted and energized her in a way she had never before known. He was able to help her connect with the source of life and happiness and hope.

As followers of Christ we are capable of being "diamonds of hope," radiating a message of encouragement that energizes those we meet and with whom we relate. What others are looking for in life is what we also are looking for. All of us in some way at various times are searching for meaning, value, and happiness in life. What happens too often is that we look in all the wrong places. We fail to realize that when we think we can get away from it all for awhile, we are taking a major part of the problem with us— ourselves. We fail to acknowledge that when we think we will find a better church, we are taking our complaints with us. What we don't like here shows up there because much of the problem is ours. We are blind when we think that a new relationship will solve our problems, because much of the difficulty lies in the patterns we develop in relating to others.

We, like the woman at the well, are thirsty. But often we don't realize how thirsty we are until someone calls it to our attention, as Jesus did for her. Once we acknowledge our need for a permanent source of refreshment and nourishment, then we are better able to see that the source, God's abiding love, is available to us wherever we are. God's care for us transcends any and all barriers we might erect.

Certainly the Samaritan woman at the well was a seeker. In her searching she discovered happiness as a by-product of being accepted and loved by a man, a Jew, and a rabbi. As a seeker she also became a witness inviting people to come and see "the man who told her everything she had ever done." Her witness was invitational. Come and see and decide if this is the Christ. We too can become witnesses inviting people to come and see, permitting them to decide if this is the Christ. They and we will discover that we are connected to springs of hope that flow to us and through us out into the desert. And the desert will bloom with the lives of other seekers who discover they are accepted and loved by the One who has loved us and poured out life to demonstrate the height and depth of that love for us.

QUESTIONS TO PONDER

1. What strengths do you see in the Samaritan woman?
2. At what points do this woman's searching and your searching intersect?
3. For what do you think the Samaritan woman was searching?
4. What surprises you about the interaction of Jesus and the Samaritan woman?
5. What are some other ways this woman might have responded to Jesus?
6. When have you been a Samaritan woman? Identify your feelings and needs.
7. When have you been Jesus to a Samaritan woman? Identify your feelings and needs.

6

SEEKING SENSE IN THE NONSENSE

LUKE 8:26–39

I SERVED AS A CHAPLAIN at Norton Psychiatric Hospital in Louisville, Kentucky, while I was a seminary student. I recall being encouraged by Wayne Oates during the introduction and orientation for that position. He urged us "to make sense out of the nonsense" in our work with patients. Having been traumatized by some situation, patients in a psychiatric hospital may say what sounds like nonsense. But it isn't. Mainly they are trying to communicate their perception of what is happening in their lives. As a result of the trauma they have experienced, they look at life through distorted lenses. Seeking to make sense out of the nonsense helps bring their experience into clearer focus and provides better understanding for the patient and for the chaplain.

According to Luke's Gospel, Jesus made a visit to a first-century psychiatric hospital (Luke 8:26–39). Perhaps on first reading or hearing this account you were tempted, as I was, to dismiss it as nonsense. The event happened so long ago and we have such limited information about the situation that it seems impossible to make any sense out of what sounds like nonsense.

However, we must not dismiss this story so quickly. By exploring this story we can meet a man who was seeking to make some sense out of the nonsense in his life. He approached Jesus for assistance in the journey. By the end of the story the man was making sense and the crowd of people who came out to see him and Jesus seem to be the insane ones.

The way Luke tells the story, Jesus took a boat ride across the Lake of Galilee toward the community of Gerasa. Apparently the city boat dock was out at the edge of the cemetery. Just as Jesus stepped off the boat, this crazy man approached him. If he weren't crazy, he certainly had some unusual habits. Luke identified him as having demons. On occasion the people of the town had tried to keep him restrained with chains—the first-century straight jacket. However, the restraints worked temporarily at best. Evidently when the seizures came, he became uncontrollable and was frightening to people. Although they put chains and iron clasps on him, he broke them with ease during the seizures. He wandered around through the hills screaming and cutting himself with stones. He walked around naked. Does this describe the normal behavior of anyone you know? The popular diagnosis for a person like this in the first century was that he had an evil spirit or was demon possessed. That was the way that people in the first century explained many situations that were abnormal and for which there seemed to be no corrective. People who were mentally retarded, emotionally disturbed, had what we now call Alzheimer's disease, or were afflicted with epilepsy were identified as being controlled by demons. No one would have anything to do with this man. The people in town not only claimed he was demon possessed, they were convinced that more than one demon was in him. They identified a different demon as the cause of each bizarre behavior.

A common belief was also that such conditions were the result of sin. Unfortunately, some people still hold similar views. In the early 1980s, a person in the Department of Education said that the mentally ill were that way because of sin and that they had been a drain on the resources of the nation. That view did not end at the end of the twentieth century.

I once knew a woman who suffered from multiple sclerosis. She was confined to her bed, except when someone lifted her from the bed to her wheelchair. One morning around eight o'clock, after her husband had departed for work and before her mother arrived to be with her for the day, she was awakened by two "friends" standing over her and praying for the demons to come out of her so she could be healed. In essence, they, like Job's friends, were accusing her of sin that had caused her to be possessed by demons. The "friends" were asked never to return unless the woman's husband was present.

I've known of other situations where values differed. What one considered acceptable action, another considered a horrible sin. In a desire to be pure and keep pure, the one who disagreed condemned the other to hell. What is redemptive about that? Although the area of condemnation is not in our God-given domain, it never keeps some fools from rushing in where angels fear to tread.

Why do you think this man was living in the cemetery? Did he choose to live there or did the community force him there? Was his residence the result of a combination of his choosing and the coercion of the community? I wonder if this man were living in the cemetery because a very important person in his life was buried there. The death of that person may have been so traumatic that he could cope in no other way than to spend more and more time in the cemetery. The death of an important person in our lives can cause us to react in some very strange, uncharacteristic, and even bizarre ways. It is not uncommon for anybody, including you and me, to become fixated on an event, situation, or condition in life. Every aspect of life comes to be filtered through and interpreted by that event or situation. Many of you have lost important people in your lives and found yourself doing strange things. I knew a woman who on several occasions prepared dinner for her and her husband and waited for him to come in from feeding the livestock. Only when he didn't come did she remember he had died. For thirty years it had been their routine to come in from their jobs in town and for her to prepare dinner while he fed the livestock. Her adjustment to his death was not immediate and automatic. Some people would have said she was crazy. She felt like she was losing her mind. But she wasn't. Her actions were understandable given her circumstances. It is possible to make sense out of nonsense.

Perhaps this man in Luke's story chose to live among the dead rather than among the living because he found it safer and easier. As long as he stayed in the burial caves no one mistreated him. Perhaps the community also felt safer with him among the tombs. In the first century, cemeteries were the places designated for habitation by mentally and emotionally disturbed people—individuals with "evil spirits." Living among the tombs gave them a place of their own, space to roam, and of course, rid society of their presence, protected the sane from the insane. Restricting disturbed people to cemeteries became such a prevalent practice that eventually anyone seen in a cemetery was automatically labeled a disturbed person. This is why I said at the outset that Jesus visited a first-century psychiatric hospital.

Jesus helped this man find the courage to master his fears by walking through them. In that way Jesus set the man free of the bondage of his fears and he was able to move back into the community of the living rather than existing out there among the dead. He must have begun to believe that he was one of the walking dead. In a sense he was.

Perhaps this man had been angered by the death of someone and had let the anger sour and become bitterness. He pretended not to hurt and began to despair. A deep sense of frustration accompanied all of this and he was driven to an emotional breakdown. One of the ways that our bodies deal with the intense stress that a loss causes is to get sick. One of the most stressful events in life is the death of a spouse. If some other stress occurs very soon after the death of a spouse, the grief is compounded and the emotional make-up of the person begins to shut out and deny feelings in an attempt to protect the person emotionally. I am amazed at times as I work with people at the intense pain they continue to carry with them because of a loss that happened long ago.

Some people respond to stress by checking out of reality. The load is more than they can bear or are willing to face. They so intensely fear what may happen that they refuse to face it. Maybe the man in the tombs had been unable to bury his dead. Maybe he was maltreated as a child. He was certainly a brokenhearted man and carried the dead around with him in his life. Whatever may have occurred earlier in his life, the picture in the Gospels is of a man whose personality had been shattered and broken to pieces. He identified himself to Jesus as Legion, which meant many. He was a broken and fragmented person with no center of focus and no cohesiveness about his life.

I wonder if this man did not also function as the whipping post for the community. They may have projected onto this man all the darkness of their lives. They may have been chaining up the parts of themselves they feared to face when they chained this man. What was frightening about him breaking his chains may have been the awareness that they could not control the negative things about themselves by hiding them or pretending they were not there. This man may have been the human scapegoat for every bad thing that happened in the community. When something was stolen, the crazy cemetery sitter was the thief. When people in the community didn't get along, it was blamed on the influence of Tombstone Tommy. By having Tombstone Tommy everyone in the community could be unaccountable and irresponsible. Someone else always caused any problems. All you had to do was take a look at Tombstone Tommy and know right away where the source of trouble was.

Now, as soon as Jesus stepped off the boat, Luke says this man met him. The wording suggests the man initiated contact with Jesus. What was he seeking, needing? In all of the nonsense that was happening in his life, he knew things were not right. He wanted to make some sense out of his life. My impression is that no one had ever approached this man with compassion, care, or interest. Look at his reaction to Jesus as soon as he sees him. He said to Jesus, "What do you want with me? For God's sake, I beg you, please don't punish me!" Isn't this an unusual response to someone he had never met? Does this response suggest that any who had dared come near this man previously had attempted to do something to him, to use him or abuse him in some way? But isn't this often our approach when we sense God getting close to us? Isn't there a residue of belief somewhere in the back of our minds that God is out to get us? I get this sense from people in their responses to me. Because I am a minister, a representative of God, they anticipate that I am going to be judgmental or condemning of them in spite of the observations they have made of me to the contrary. Maybe it is best explained in the announcement a preschooler made to her parents. I had arranged to visit with this family late one afternoon. The parents had told the children that the preacher was coming to visit. I parked in their driveway and as I got out of the car, the preschooler saw me through the window of her room and announced to her mother, "Mommy, the creature is coming! The creature is coming!" In some ways, the man in Luke's story saw Jesus and felt like "the creature was coming."

In response to the man's question, Jesus got personal. He asked, "What is your name?" Here is a frightened and apparently frightening individual. He is the outcast of outcasts. Luke portrays a foreboding human being who runs around naked, ripping off chains and iron clasps, a kind of first-century Incredible Hulk. When Jesus meets him, he wants to know his name. What a novel idea! Since he was a person, Jesus treated him personally by asking his name. And the man said, "My name is Tombstone Tommy, Digger Dan, Burying Burt, Screaming Sam, Seizure Steve." His name was all of these and more. According to Luke the man said, "My name is Legion," because there were many demons in him. Here was a man with multiple personalities.

To name something, to name oneself, to name how one is feeling is to begin to gain control over whatever or whomever is named. Even though the man said his name was Legion, meaning there were many fragmented parts to him, he was beginning to gain some control over those many parts. But notice what happened next. We are told that the man kept begging Jesus not to send the evil spirits out of that region.

Wasn't this a strange request? Why would one as troubled as this man, who apparently believed that demons or evil spirits were the cause of his condition, plead with Jesus or anyone else to do nothing about the situation? I think it had to do with the issue of change in the man's life. I am continually astounded at the damaging relationships that people refuse to do anything about because they are afraid of the unknown results that will come following the change. People get a certain amount of emotional payoff by holding on to their resentments or they punish themselves by wallowing in their guilt rather than doing anything constructive about getting rid of their resentments or their guilt. Here was a man, crazy as he was, who knew how to function out in the cemetery. He knew that people expected him to scream and mourn, cut himself and walk around naked. Were he to get over whatever was the source of such behavior, he was not sure if he would know how to act or how people would respond to him.

I picked up a hitchhiker once, a man who lived in the community where we lived. I had seen him on several occasions. He was shabbily dressed, dirty, had a strong body odor. His appearance was rough and disturbing. The odor of alcohol was strong. His first words after getting in the car were "No harm in me. No harm in me." In the brief time that he was in the car he repeated that phrase several times. I had the impression that many people had shied away from him on various occasions, had treated him harshly, and said damning things to him. His statement was an attempt to put me at ease from the outset that I had nothing to fear in him.

I wonder if there was a sense in which the man Jesus met in Gerasa felt something like that. He was not there to harm anyone. There is no indication in the accounts of this event that the man had ever attempted to do harm to anyone other than himself.

One of the troubling aspects of this story is that in some way, a large herd of pigs was drowned. The writers say the demons or evil spirits entered the pigs and the pigs ran over the cliff, fell into the lake, and drowned. Perhaps the noise being made as the man resisted Jesus frightened the hogs. Some believed that the only way to destroy evil spirits was to drown them. Perhaps when the pigs ran into the water and the man appeared well, those watching drew the conclusion that demons had entered the pigs. (Of course, the loss of his pigs must have upset the man who owned them.) Incidentally, this part of the story suggests that this was a Gentile area since the Jews considered pigs unclean.

The men who had been taking care of the pigs ran into town to tell the people what had happened. As is so characteristic of people, many came out to see the sights. When they arrived they saw the man sitting there by Jesus, clothed and in his right mind, and they were all afraid. Now, isn't that a strange reaction? Here is a man who had been running and screaming through the cemetery and cutting himself and their reaction had been to tie him down. Now that he is normal they are afraid. Afraid of what? Did they fear that this man in his right mind might now retaliate against them for all they had done to him? Were they afraid that they had related so long to this man as sick that they did not know how to relate to him now that he was well? That does happen. We fit people into molds. When they begin making changes in their lives, we have trouble because we are unsure how to relate to them. This can happen in every family when children grow up. As they become their own persons, they make decisions and relate in ways that are different from when parents could make them do things their way. There often is much fear in such homes.

Another unusual response is that the people wanted Jesus to leave the territory. This gives us the clue as to whom they feared—

Jesus more than the healed man. Anyone who had the power to heal the town crazy was a threat to them. He could bring about change that they were not sure they could face and handle. They asked Jesus to leave and he left. Just like that. No resistance. On another occasion Jesus instructed his disciples that if people in a town were not receptive to them, they should shake the dust off their feet and move on. Here Jesus seemed very willing to take his own advice.

The man wanted to go with Jesus but Jesus asked him to go back home and tell his family how much God had done for him. The man did that, and people throughout Decapolis, a ten-city area, were amazed when they heard what had happened.

In spite of our supposed sophistication, insight, and understanding, how differently do we treat the disturbed people of our society compared with the way the people treated Legion? Where do we put the disturbed people of our society? With what places and institutions are they identified? On one end of the spectrum are prisons and jails. Have you seen some of these places? In many cases, the people kept in these places would welcome the opportunity to live among the tombs in a cemetery. And there are those who want us to build more facilities like these. I'm willing to grant that this may be at the extreme end of the spectrum.

What about some of the places and conditions under which people work today? Do some of these qualify as dwelling places for the disturbed? Our choice of words may be more revealing than we realize. Sometimes we describe our work environment as bedlam—the word is derived from a notorious English insane asylum. We often speak of the hassle that life is. As we seek to move up in the organization for which we work, disorientation seems to be a price we are willing to pay.

And what answers do we offer for these situations? I'm not sure we do much better than those in the first century. Those people chained the disturbed ones in their midst. We observe, "If you want something done, give the assignment to a very busy person. He'll get the job done." "Joe will kill himself to meet his quotas.

Give him that territory where we need to improve sales." "Sue is a real go-getter. She'll do anything to get the job done. Put her in charge of that unmanageable division." In the movie *The Firm*, a new lawyer is hired and paid a lucrative salary. Later he learns that no one ever leaves the firm alive. He learns of obvious, serious improprieties, but all employees and their families are chained to the firm.

The man identified in the Gospels as the demoniac was no more destructive of himself and his society than are people in our society who are also victimized. The difference: our sickness is a bit more sophisticated. His harm may have had more physical dimensions with cuts and bruises to show for it. Ours may be more emotional that eventually shows a physical dimension in heart disease or a weary mind or destroyed relationships. Chains and stones may have been used on him or by him. We use schedules, promotions, budgets, awards, prestige, status, and memberships.

The man asked Jesus, "What do you want with me? Why are you here, Jesus?" That's an important question at a deep level. What does Jesus have to do with my work? I take care of my business during the week and deal with God's business on Sunday. What does Jesus have to do with my business, my family, or my recreation? What does Jesus have to do with how I work or my sense of drivenness? What is Jesus doing here?

Welton Gaddy calls attention to a statement from Lord Melbourne, who served as British Prime Minister. On one occasion he stormed out of an evangelical meeting being held in his church and loudly commented, "This has come to a pretty pass when religion is made to invade the sphere of private life."[1] What is Jesus doing here?

The first thing Jesus did for this man was to be present to him by being personal. He asked him his name. Then after Jesus stayed there and helped the man integrate the parts of his personality that had been all mixed up while he was trying to live among the dead, we find the man clothed and in his right mind. In the last scene of the story the man had buried the dead and wanted to go back to the community of the living. Jesus suggested that he go home to his friends and tell them what God had done.

Here was a man searching, seeking, wanting to make sense out of the nonsense in his life. There seemed to be no one willing to interact with him, care for him, and treat him like a human being, no one until Jesus stepped off the boat. And the man approached Jesus. Maybe the man approached everyone who ever got close to him the same way, but was always rejected. Frankly, it is amazing this man would approach any other human being, given the way he had been treated for years. But it does reveal that when people's lives are wrapped in pain and torment, they run any risk in an effort to get relief. Here was a seeker whose life made no sense until he met Jesus. And Jesus treated him differently. When he was treated differently, he began to behave differently. Others treated him like an animal and he lived like an animal. Jesus treated him as person, a human being, and he began to act like a human being, dressed and in his right mind.

Jesus accepted this brokenhearted man by taking the time to be with him. He showed him that it is appropriate to bury the dead, whatever in us is dead, and move on through the darkness to the light on the other side. Presence, support, affirmation, empathy, and love are all personal traits. Only people can give these gifts. Often it is through people giving these gifts to others that people discover the goodness and the healing of God's grace in their lives.

QUESTIONS TO PONDER

1. Can you identify some of what makes you "crazy"?

2. Where are the tombs for you?

3. What is some of the nonsense in your life?

4. What nonsense do you need to make sense out of?

5. What is frightening about the possibility of Jesus putting you in your right mind?

6. What would your life be like if you were in your right mind?

7

SEEKING SECURITY

THE BIBLE IS A TREASURY OF LIFE. The vignettes of people's lives contained in the Bible are rich. As we read these stories, hear about them, or act them out we can project ourselves into them and discover how they are also vignettes of our lives. The intersections of our stories with these stories are often closer to reality than we like. We may discover more about ourselves than we really want to see.

In the Gospels of Matthew, Mark, and Luke are similar accounts of a conversation between a particular man and Jesus. While the accounts are similar, they are not identical. By examining all three Gospels we are able to develop a composite impression of this man. Although his name is not given, he is identified as the rich ruler. All three writers disclose near the end of their accounts that this was a wealthy man. It is Matthew who describes him as young and Luke who infers that he was a ruler by writing about his piety and his wealth. In the context of Luke's Gospel, a ruler referred to a member either of the local synagogue council or of the Sanhedrin, not to a prince or a king. He was not someone who had or would have political clout and dominion over a community or a region.

The manner in which he approached Jesus indicates that he was a somewhat independent and courageous person. He was at a point of searching and seeking in his life. There is no way to know exactly what prompted his seeking. There are times when our lives seem well ordered and moving smoothly. Other times we have lots of questions. We wonder where we are going and what the outcome will be of all of our thoughts, insights, struggles, and understanding. We wonder if there is meaning in what we are doing and experiencing.

Something prompted this kind of seeking in this young man. He seems to have been asking, "What meaning is there in my life? Is there more to life than working, eating, and sleeping? How can I be fulfilled?" I suggest this because of the question he asked, "What must I do to receive eternal life?" This is an ultimate question. This is one of many ways of asking, "When my life is over will it have made any difference that I have lived?" Or are we like so many people listed in Genesis who were born, begot children, and died?

When Jesus responded to this man's question about eternal life with the instruction that he live out the commandments of love for fellow human beings, the man said he had been doing that from his youth onward. It was his way of saying, "I have tried living in the proper relationship to people, but life is still empty for me, something is missing. I don't feel complete or whole." Note that Jesus said nothing about the man's relationship with God, omitting any comment about the first four commandments. Did that mean they were unimportant? Perhaps Jesus did not think they applied to this man's situation. Was Jesus focusing enough on God? Of course! The fulfillment of the last six commandments presupposed the importance and relevance of the first four. Jesus knew that no person could love his neighbor as himself if he did not love God with all of his heart, mind, and soul. However, it was not necessary for Jesus to say that in every context or to every person who engaged him in conversation about ultimate matters.

Here, in a most important situation where a man has asked Jesus about receiving eternal life, Jesus made no reference to God.

In reading the Gospel writers' accounts of the conversation between the rich ruler and Jesus, there is so much that isn't said. Surely, these two talked about more than what Matthew, Mark, and Luke tell.

It was one o'clock in the afternoon late in September in 1962. I was in study hall on the second floor of Monticello High School. The health teacher/basketball coach, Joe Harper, was in charge of study hall. About midway through the period he called me up to the desk and asked if I were planning to try out for the basketball team that year. I told him, "No. I have a job and I'm working every afternoon after school." He said, "You can work the rest of your life." Was he ever right about that! He added, "I'm working on the insurance papers for the team and I was just wondering if you were going to try out this year." I reaffirmed my negative answer. Of course a lot more was being said than was being said. By saying, "No," I was saying to the coach, "Are you crazy? I tried out last year and didn't make it. Do you think I want to put myself through all of that hard work, all that running, dribbling, and shooting? And that rope jumping. I can't jump rope. It's humiliating. Why should I get out there and make a fool of myself again in front of guys who are so much better than I and then have you tell me that I didn't make the team. So, my answer is no." I was saying a lot that I was not saying aloud. But so was the coach. That afternoon as I thought about what he had said to me, I realized, "Maybe all I have to do to make the team is to try out. Why would he want to know about my decision while he is working on the insurance forms if he does not already think I have the ability to make the team?" Well, I did try out for the team and made it. I spent two years on the junior varsity, one year as a substitute and one year as a starter. My senior year I started every game at the pivot position for the varsity. And I'm glad I made the team; otherwise I would have had few illustrations for sermons and books during the last thirty-five years. A lot more went on in that conversation between Joe Harper and me than was spoken.

I suspect that a lot more went on in the conversation between the rich ruler and Jesus than has been written down for us. What we seem to have is the nugget of truth after the attending setting has been washed away. This story was told and retold innumerable times after Jesus' death and was not written down for at least thirty years. Most likely in that length of time, some parts of the story were omitted and what we have left is the punch line. How many times have we heard stories that really were valuable but later could only remember the punch lines? On other occasions we could remember most of the story, make up what we couldn't remember to embellish it, but couldn't tell the story because we couldn't remember the punch line.

Every time I read this conversation between Jesus and the rich ruler, I am amazed with what precision and insight Jesus got to the heart of life with this man. I wonder if Jesus had seen this man on other occasions or had other encounters with him. Palestine was a small territory with a small population 2,000 years ago. Galilee was one section of that country where Jesus spent most of his ministry. Had Jesus seen this man and observed some things about his lifestyle, his attitudes, and his view of life? That is possible and probable. Or maybe the man said other things to Jesus in this encounter that gave Jesus clues about the man's perspective on life. Otherwise, why did Jesus zero in on the wealth issue with this man?

This was not a pet issue with Jesus and he did not give pat answers to people's questions. In all the vignettes the Gospel writers record about Jesus' encounters with people, no two conversations are the same, no two needs are the same, and Jesus nowhere gives two people the same instruction. The rich ruler is the only person Jesus tells to sell all that he had, give it to the poor, and come follow him. Jesus did not stereotype or pigeonhole people. Just because a person was wealthy did not mean that person was possessed by his possessions. There is no evidence that Jesus prejudged anyone, but his hunch and assessment about the rich man were right on target, because he was unwilling to let his possessions go. How well Jesus could listen to people with what has been identified as the third ear.

How often we talk in riddles! There are times when we fear being hurt or rejected. We toss out little hints about ourselves to a person and if those aren't batted down, we reveal a bit more of ourselves, take a little greater risk in the relationship. The result is that trust begins to develop. The more trust evolves, the more risk we take.

This vignette from Jesus' ministry has richness beyond the wealth of the rich ruler. It contains a model of Jesus' ministry. In a typical encounter, through engaging conversation, often initiated by the other person but precipitated by some action, statement, or activity of Jesus, Jesus would establish a relationship with a person. He sought to learn and know as much about the person as possible. Then, he focused attention and responses to the person in a way that highlighted how God's presence, love, and mercy applied in this person's life. Jesus did not need a step-by-step plan to relate to people. Rather he listened and learned about a person. He never told two people the same thing. Why? People are created in the image of God. They are unique and no two have exactly the same needs. Therefore, God's love does not come to them or apply in their lives in identical ways.

What Jesus' conversation with the rich ruler says to us is that we need to know as much about the life and spirit of Jesus as possible. The best way I know to do that is to read, reread, and reflect on all the information, responses, and interactions Jesus had with people that the Gospel writers have recorded for us. As we do this, we will gain new insight into Jesus and his approach. We will discover creative, engaging ways to develop relationships and see how the good news applies to the needs of people we know. Relationship with God permeates and undergirds the entire encounter of Jesus with the rich ruler.

A wise man reached the outskirts of a little town and settled under a tree for the night. A citizen of the town came running to him, urging, "The stone! The stone! Give me the precious stone!"

"What stone?"

"Last night the Lord appeared to me in a dream," said the citizen, "and told me that if I went to the edge of town at dusk I would find a wise man who would give me a precious stone that would make me rich forever."

The wise man rummaged through his bag and pulled out a stone. "He probably meant this one," he said, as he handed the stone over to the villager. I found it on a forest path several days ago. You certainly can have it."

The man gazed at the stone in wonder. It was a diamond, probably the largest diamond in the world. It was as large as a person's head. He took the diamond and walked away. All night he tossed about in bed, unable to sleep. At the crack of dawn the next day he woke the wise man and said, "Give me the wealth that makes it possible for you to give this diamond away so easily."[1]

The rich ruler in the Gospels is not that wealthy—not in spirit. He's a good man who's filthy rich, asking a sincere question about meaning in life: "What must I do to inherit eternal life?" When Jesus invites him to become a traveling disciple—after he does the one thing lacking in his life, to sell all he has and give it to the poor—the rich man, Luke writes, "became very sad, because he was a man of great wealth."

But he is not wealthy enough to give it all away. He is spiritually bankrupt but unwilling to ackowledge it. Perhaps he's enough of a seeker that if Jesus just invites him to become a follower and a generous benefactor who underwrites the expenses of the ministry, he could do it, and even make some sacrifices.

But Jesus does not ask him to make sacrifices that will enable him to continue in his identity as a rich man. Jesus invites him to give it all away, which will mean giving away his old identity—the way others think of him and the way he thinks of himself. He's not just a man. He's a rich man. The anxiety about the future and personal security that plagues most people is not his to deal with, for he is a person of great wealth.

Jesus' invitation is so radical that it does not sound like an invitation at all to the rich man. It sounds out of the question, totally divorced from reality. So with great sadness . . . he walks away. And then Jesus runs after him, saying, "Wait a minute! You have a lot to contribute to my ministry. Why, you can pay for everything I would ever need in my ministry. Surely, we can work out something that would be agreeable." Of course, that is not what Jesus said, but perhaps this is what we might say if we were in a similar situation.

Imagine the story reading like this: "Jesus said to him, 'You still lack one thing. Sell everything you have and give it to the poor, and you will have treasure in heaven. Then come, follow me.' When the rich man heard this, he grinned from ear to ear, and said, 'Okay! Sure, Jesus, no problem. That's a small price for being with you and having eternal life.' Although he was a man of great wealth, he immediately sent word for all that he owned to be sold and used to feed the hungry and house the homeless. Then, with a lightness of heart and a new spring in his step, he walked away with Jesus—who was also grinning from ear to ear—no longer a rich man but a new man, and strangely enough, feeling wealthier than ever."

Giving away all you have or giving away the world's largest diamond requires nonchalance toward possessions that rises out of a deep inner freedom. We can only give away if we are detached from what we have. If we are attached to it—and that's the way to describe it, for our possessions are not attached to us—then we hold on and will not let go.

In the 1800s, a tourist from the United States visited the famous Polish Rabbi Hafez Hayyim. He was astonished to see that the rabbi's home was only a simple room filled with books. The only furniture was a table and a bench.

"Rabbi, where is your furniture?" asked the tourist.

"Where is yours?" replied Hafez.

"Mine? But I'm only a visitor here."

"So am I," said the rabbi.[2]

And so are we. As visitors here we need to turn loose whatever we're attached to so we can develop relationships with people we encounter. It is in these relationships that we will get our clearest glimpses of God. Through these relationships we will best witness the grace, love, and acceptance of God. Only through relating to and knowing a person because we love and care for that person will we be able to discern how God's love modeled in Jesus applies to that person's needs. Only through loving this person will we establish enough trust and credibility for the person to consider allowing God's presence, love, and grace to flow into his or her life and then on to others. We see this entire way of bearing witness to God modeled for us in Jesus' encounter with the rich ruler.

The rich ruler was seeking God. His story reveals the direction he chose at probably the most important intersection he came to in life. We need to allow our lives to intersect with the life of Christ and at those intersections we need to stop, look, and listen to the flood of God's grace that is poured out to all who will receive. To receive the grace of God is to detach ourselves from whatever we are attached to. Then we become new people who are strangely wealthier than we have ever been.

QUESTIONS TO PONDER

1. To what are you attached?

2. What do you have to do to inherit eternal life?

3. Where does your life intersect with the life of the rich ruler?

4. What is God saying to you at this intersection?

5. If you were Jesus, how would you respond to the rich ruler?

6. If you met Jesus today, what would you need him to say to you?

8

A PUSHY SEEKER[1]

MATTHEW 15:21–28

MANY YEARS AGO the publishers of *Reader's Digest* developed an idea that was popularly received. They developed the *Reader's Digest Condensed Books*. Many people have read one or more of those books because they could get the basic meaning of a particular book without having to wade through all of the pages of the original.

Many high school students are familiar with the Cliffs Notes series. These summarize in a few pages the plot, subplot, themes, and character development of major literary works that are required reading in many classes. A few years ago, *Reader's Digest* published a condensed version of the Bible. Reviews were not so positive. Some thought it was a travesty that passages of Scripture would be omitted in this version, which suggested that these passages were not as important as others were. Some protested strongly because they said they believed the whole Bible, and someone ought not to be tampering with Scripture, picking and choosing to publish some passages while omitting others.

What do you think? More to the point, what do you practice? Who does not have his or her own condensed version of Scripture? Do we not all have favorite passages of Scripture?

When we turn for guidance, are there certain passages to which we turn? When was the last time you sought inspiration from the Book of Numbers or received comfort and guidance from the "begat" section of Genesis? When did you last include Habakkuk or Nahum, Titus or Philemon in your reading of Scripture?

Many of us read from the PCV translation of the Bible, Personally Condensed Version. I wonder if the story that Matthew tells about a Syrophoenician woman is in anyone's personally condensed version of the Bible. I doubt it. I even had difficulty finding much in the commentaries on this particular passage. It is a difficult, troubling passage of Scripture and we really would rather avoid it. There are plenty of other passages we prefer to read.

Part of the struggle readers have with this story is that it does not portray Jesus as he is usually portrayed, in a positive light. Maybe we should leave the story alone. When you finish reading this chapter, you may agree. The story has both compelling and repelling qualities. I'm going to wrestle with the repelling qualities first. Maybe that's just my way of getting the hard part behind me. Maybe that's so I can enjoy the compelling parts more. Maybe it is nothing more than here I am six paragraphs into this chapter, and I must start somewhere. Anyway, here goes.

Both Matthew and Mark refer to this event in Jesus' ministry, with some differences. Exploring both accounts provides insight and understanding. This story, identified by many as Jesus' encounter with the Syrophoenician woman, is one of only two or three recorded circumstances where Jesus had any involvement with Gentiles. The event took place the only time we are told that Jesus was outside of Palestine during his ministry; supposedly this is the only time he was off Jewish soil other than in his early childhood when Joseph and Mary took him to Egypt.

Often when we read the Bible we are left to read between the lines. Matthew probably intended to place this story where he did in his Gospel. A friend once commented to me that he did not think writing was such a difficult task. He said, "All you do is put one word after another." I told him I agreed but the difficulty I had was deciding which word was to follow which word. Since Matthew did not attempt to give a chronological account of Jesus' ministry, he had to decide which event in Jesus' ministry he would place after which event. In the section preceding the story that is the basis for this chapter, Matthew clearly showed that there was nothing anyone ate that was defiling. This story states with certainty that there are no people who are off limits to Jesus. Mark, in describing this event, says that Jesus was attempting to get some time away from the demands people were making on him. Mark says he went to someone's house because he did not want anyone to know where he was. But he could not stay hidden (Mark 7:24).

A woman approached Jesus. Matthew identifies her as a Canaanite, meaning she probably was from a more rural section in that region. Mark says she was a Gentile from Syria in the region of Phoenicia. This is how she became identified as the Syrophoenician woman. This woman may have been the most aggressive woman who lived in the first century. Often we read a passage of Scripture like this and do not recognize what unusual events are being described because we are oblivious to the cultural norms of that time.

Several factors make this a most unusual event. First, a woman never approached a man. Second, if a man approached a woman in public, the woman was expected not to look at him and was not to respond in conversation with him. Third, the woman in this story was a Gentile and should have kept away from the home of an observant Jew if you follow Mark's account, and kept away from a Jewish man, Jesus, if you follow Matthew's account. Certainly she should never have sought an unescorted audience with a Jewish man, especially if she were going to ask him a favor. Not only did this woman approach Jesus, she spoke out to him and cleverly and incautiously talked back to Jesus while asking for his help. This is outrageous! Yet, she does all of this with tenacity and wit. This woman is on a mission—a crusade even—on behalf of her daughter, and she will let nothing, no custom, no expectation, no rule stand in her way. She was a pushy woman! Does that assessment trouble you? What is it about aggressive people that make us uncomfortable? Is the discomfort intensified if the aggressive person is a woman? We have some cultural norms ourselves that we expect people to follow. The first century Middle Eastern culture had certain norms and expectations. Whether they were written down or not, everyone knew what they were. A person ignored those "rules" at great risk to her life.

Why was the Syrophoenician woman so aggressive? She was dealing with a matter of life or death. She was convinced that the condition of her daughter was so bad that the girl would die. This mother was willing to take any risk in the hope of finding healing for her daughter. Every parent who has had a child in a life-threatening situation can identify with this behavior.

The woman said that her daughter had a demon and was in a terrible condition. What a thing to say, that your child has a demon! But in the first century, various mental and emotional difficulties were commonly attributed to being caused by demons. It is cruel for people to make such a diagnosis today because it suggests that people who are mentally ill are that way because they have in some way collaborated with evil or the condition has come on them as punishment for some misdeed.

Here was a woman willing to break every social custom if necessary to get help for her daughter. Although Jesus had not been to any Gentile territory during his ministry before this day, his reputation must have preceded him. Otherwise, why did this woman approach him as soon as he set foot in her town?

There does seem to be a "safe" dimension to Jesus' personality that enabled people to open up to him in ways they never would with anyone else. Maybe Jesus conveyed that immediately. Maybe this woman sensed something like that. I don't know. It's purely conjecture. As troubling as it may be for some that this aggressive woman initiated conversation with Jesus with the specific intent of soliciting help from him, all of that pales for me compared to Jesus' response to her.

I should say, Jesus' lack of response. The woman makes herself completely vulnerable to Jesus. Who knows how long it took her to get up the courage to approach Jesus? Having decided that, imagine how nervous she felt as she anticipated what she was going to say. Perhaps she played out the conversation in her mind, anticipating all of the possible responses Jesus might make to her and how she would respond. Of all of the responses recorded in the Gospels that Jesus made to people, to their questions and their requests, his response to this woman is most troubling. She said to him, "Have mercy on me, sir! My daughter has a demon and is in a terrible condition" (Matthew 15:22). And how did Jesus respond? He ignored her. Matthew's description is worded this way—he ignored her.

This non-response, ignoring this woman, is disturbing. First, it is so out of character for Jesus. Jesus was accused of a lot of things. He was accused of partying too much. He was accused of not keeping all of the religious rules. He was accused of associating with all the wrong people. He was accused of being a glutton and a drunkard. He was accused of having no control over his disciples, allowing them to roam free, even to work on the Sabbath. He was accused of paying attention to the unimportant people. He was accused of spending time with anybody and everybody who came along. But he was never accused of ignoring people. And yet in this situation he ignores this woman. Second, not only is it out of character, but also it is disturbing because of what being ignored means. To be ignored means I do not matter. Whether I exist or not is of no meaning or value. Whether I live or die does not matter. Was Jesus saying it did not matter whether this woman's daughter lived or died? Was Jesus saying it did not matter whether this woman's daughter was in a terrible condition? If he were, that is most disturbing because if Jesus is saying that to this woman, he may also say it to me. How contrary that is to my image and understanding of Jesus!

The disciples sought expediency. They wanted to be done with the matter. They thought the easiest, quickest, and best solution was just to send the woman away. She was making too much noise, calling too much attention to them. They were convinced that if Jesus would just tell the woman to leave, that would solve the problem. Why they thought that a woman who had gone to so much trouble would just quietly leave at Jesus' request is beyond me. The stakes were too high and she already had risked too much to back down now.

Jesus' comment to his disciples is helpful, but not very. He said, "I have been sent only to the lost sheep of the people of Israel" (Matthew 15:24). It is helpful because Jesus is clear about his ministry and mission. He was to establish ministry with the people of Israel who then were to share God's love and good news with others beginning in Jerusalem and Judea but spreading to the "uttermost parts of the world." But even this statement is troublesome because it has an exclusionary tone to it. Was Jesus prioritizing his ministry in order to establish the work he was going to do? Was he saying that his area of focus was to be with Israel, at least for awhile?

Apparently this Canaanite woman, who had just been ignored, was overhearing this conversation between Jesus and his disciples. She did not know about all that stuff related to Jesus' ministry and him going to the lost sheep of Israel. What she did know was that her daughter was in trouble and she needed help. So the woman fell at Jesus' feet and begged him, "Help me, sir! Please help me."

I do not know if Jesus was just having a bad day or what, but his response to her again is disturbing. Having first ignored her, then Jesus said, "It is not right to take the children's food and throw it to the dogs" (Matthew 15:26). What did he mean? Was he calling the lost people of Israel children and the Canaanite woman and her daughter dogs? I certainly hope not. Was Jesus suggesting that to offer God's good news to the Gentiles would be like throwing it to the dogs? Surely not!

There is evidence that a large Jewish population was located north of the Galilean border in the political territories of Tyre and Sidon. There is reason to believe that Jesus was on his way to minister to that group of people. With that clearly as his focus, he resisted any effort by anyone to distract him from his objective. While that is commendable, still his response to this woman seems demeaning and uncaring, at least on the surface.

I do not know what you think about this woman. I do not know how you respond to her aggressiveness. I do not know what your preconceived ideas are about women. But I can tell you this— I want this woman on my side. She was persistent and refused to be ignored. She refused to accept no for an answer. She is one of the most effective advocates of an oppressed person depicted anywhere. Her daughter, oppressed by illness, was in need of healing. This woman kept seeking the help she needed from the one she was convinced could help her. Who of us would not love to be able to think on our feet as quickly as this woman did? When Jesus made his statement about throwing food to the dogs, she shot back at him that even dogs get the leftovers that fall from the master's table. It was her way of saying, "Look, I'm not asking for a seven-course meal. I will gladly receive what is left after all the others have had their fill." What was Jesus to say? I get the feeling from how Matthew tells this story that Jesus had never met anyone quite like this woman. No one had been so persistent and so tough with him. Jesus' responses to others had at times been firm, confrontational, and seemed to leave some people nearly speechless. This is the only dialogue where I sense Jesus being nearly speechless. But then Jesus said that the woman's persistence was evidence of her faith, her confidence that he really could do something significant for her daughter. He said that kind of confidence and faith brings healing, and her daughter was made well.

By the way Matthew has ordered his writing, this persistent, believing Gentile woman from the rural countryside is portrayed in sharp contrast to the unbelieving Jewish learned men who were Pharisees and scribes in the city of Jerusalem. This woman was a seeker of the highest order. She was seeking help and care for her daughter as well as for herself. She was willing to risk ridicule, rejection, and public condemnation to express her need to the one she was convinced could help her.

This woman symbolizes a need in all of us. We all need God's kindness, care, healing, and help. Whether we are unlearned country folks or sophisticated city slickers, we all need God's love and grace. And this woman symbolizes for us that people who are oppressed need relief from their misery. They are not to be ignored, but acknowledged and helped.

All of us need to base our faith in a God who can change things for the better. It is almost as if the Syrophoenician woman taught Jesus something about God of which Jesus was unaware. That's pretty hard for us to imagine! It is nearly impossible to wrap our minds around that picture of Jesus. I tell you, this is one of the most difficult biblical stories there is. For too long, too many of us have kept it out of our personally condensed version of Scripture. It is both a repelling and a compelling story. I'd say it is time for us to include it, read it, wrestle and struggle with it, and see what blessing this passage will give us before we are finished with it, or rather, before this story is finished with us.

QUESTIONS TO PONDER

1. How do you respond to the Syrophoenician woman?

2. What attracts you to this woman?

3. What repels you from this woman?

4. How is Jesus portrayed differently in this story from how he is typically depicted?

5. If this were the only information you had about Jesus, what would be your impressions and conclusions about him?

6. What does this story suggest about God?

9

A SHORT SEEKER

LUKE 19:1–10

I WAS THREE YEARS OLD. The pastor was R. E. Sasser. He stood me on the communion table at the beginning of the evening worship service and asked me to sing "Zacchaeus Was a Wee Little Man." I sang it. Apparently the minister of music heard me and got the word out. The word has preceded me wherever I have gone. One of the first things the minister of music said to me during a pastor search process was, "We never ask the pastor to sing a solo here." I think he thought he was putting me at ease. I thought, "Oh, no. Someone from Stubenville Baptist Church has already called and gotten the word to people in this church about me." That time in 1950 was the first time and the last I was asked to sing a solo.

From that early experience in my life to now I have had a strong affection for Zacchaeus. I'm sure part of the reason is that the song about Zacchaeus helped me to remember him. But as I have grown older and explored the Bible, especially focusing on Jesus and his ministry, I have become even more appreciative of Zacchaeus and of how Jesus responded to him.

In telling about Zacchaeus, Luke gives one of the most descriptive accounts of a seeker recorded in Scripture. Luke writes, "He was trying to see Jesus." Is that not what all of us are doing or need to do? Are we not all seekers, trying to see Jesus? Let's take a look at Zacchaeus. We'll discover he looks a lot like us or that we look a lot like him.

Only Luke tells this story. What he tells isn't much. It is so characteristic of Luke to tell a story like this one—of a person shut out, an outcast from society and culture. No one wanted to have anything to do with Zacchaeus. He was the middleman of all middlemen. He was caught in the middle and despised by people on both sides.

Tradition has said Zacchaeus was a short man and that he climbed a tree so he could see over the crowd. The solo I sang at age three and that many others have sung has passed on this tradition:

> *Zacchaeus was a wee little man,*
> *And a wee little man was he;*
> *He climbed up in a sycamore tree,*
> *For the Lord he wanted to see.*

The word arrangement in the text makes it possible for Jesus to have been the short man, but we do not like to consider that. Such thoughts alter our image of the Messiah too much. Only short people seem to be comfortable with the idea of a short Messiah.

Whether or not Zacchaeus was short physically, he was short in a lot of other ways. He was short on respect. He was short on acceptance. He was short on reputation. He was short on integrity. He was short on being trusted. He was short on friends. There is no way to know if all of Zacchaeus' shortness was justified.

Zacchaeus was a revenuer, an Internal Revenue agent. You know how you feel about the Internal Revenue Service around April 15th, don't you? You may agree with Albert Einstein, brilliant man that he was, who said, "The hardest thing in the world to understand is the income tax." Someone else quipped, "It is an axiom that there are just two certainties in life: death and taxes, but at least death doesn't get worse every time Congress is in session!" These expressions are mild compared to how many Jews felt about Zacchaeus! Zacchaeus was a chief tax collector in charge of the Jericho office. He had several people who worked for him collecting taxes from the Jews for the Roman government.

Jericho was an important trade center, and because of its warmth the Herods made it their winter capital. Jericho had world-famous balsam groves that perfumed the air for miles around. The Romans carried dates and balsam from Jericho to worldwide trade and fame. Because of the travel that passed through Jericho, the city was one of the great taxation centers in Palestine.

The Romans collected personal and property taxes themselves, but farmed out the collection of customs on goods to tax collectors. The tax collectors earned their livelihood from the customs tax they collected by charging more taxes than they paid to the Roman government. If the tax collectors were to have any income, they had to take it from the collected revenue. But they had better not shortchange Rome. Rome did not care how much the taxmen collected as long as Rome got what it levied. Jericho was a prosperous place for tax collectors because of the volume of business conducted there. Apparently dishonesty was prevalent among tax collectors. They were generally more affluent than others in the community and that added to the suspicion and hostility other citizens had toward them.

The Roman government ruled the Mediterranean world at that time by stationing troops in provinces throughout their conquered lands. Each province had a governor who was directly responsible to Caesar. The Romans wanted to have as little day-to-day dealings as possible with the people who were native to a province, so they had local people collect the custom taxes.

Do you see how such an arrangement immediately set up a hostile situation? A man wants to earn a living. He observes that collecting taxes is an adequate, if not lucrative, job. He begins collecting the custom taxes and is spit on from both sides. He's a Jew, a native of the land and the Roman officer to whom he gives the collected revenue doesn't want to have anything to do with him. All he wants is an exact accounting of the funds; bring in the money and leave. And the people paying the custom taxes don't want to have anything to do with him. He is a traitor. He has sold out to the occupied forces. He is aiding and abetting the enemy. They isolate him. They may have to pay the taxes, but they don't have to like the man who collects them. This is what the setting and climate were like where Zacchaeus worked. A person would have to become callused to work in such an environment. He probably would develop a stern, hard, impenetrable outer shell, never revealing the hurt he felt from the words and attitudes of people treating him like an outcast or like one with a plague.

We know very little about Zacchaeus, but we know immediately upon meeting him in Luke's story that he was despised and rejected. The biblical writers categorize the tax collectors with the sinners, indicating that as far as the people were concerned they were one and the same. Although Zacchaeus' name means "pure" or "righteous one," people treated him according to his profession rather than his name. Zacchaeus was guilty by association. Frederick Buechner describes Zacchaeus as "a sawed-off little social disaster with a big bank account and a crooked job . . ."[1] Zacchaeus was a lonely, abused man. He may have been wealthy, but he was not happy. Even if he was honest, he was abused by his fellow citizens. They treated him as a social outcast because of his profession.

Zacchaeus climbed the tree for a variety of reasons. He climbed it for his own protection. The fact that he was mingling in the crowd reveals either his courage or his desperation. For Zacchaeus to be in the crowd gave the people the opportunity to spit on him, kick him, push, shove, and bruise him. A crowd has no conscience and will often do things that individuals would never consider. People in a crowd will take advantage of the opportunity to do something for which no one will hold them accountable. Were I Zacchaeus, knowing how people felt about me, I'd try to get out of people's reach. I'd climb a tree too.

That Zacchaeus climbed a tree to see Jesus certainly identifies something of what Zacchaeus' emotional state was. He felt isolated and lonely and was saying with body language, "It's lonely here!"

Have you ever said a similar thing with body language? With empty eyes and drawn faces you and I have said, "It's lonely here." Many of us are saying it right now. Emotionally, it is January in our lives. Although January is the first month of the year, it is one of the darker months emotionally. There may be some correlation between the darkness we feel in our lives and physical darkness that occurs in January. Although the number of minutes of daylight increases from December, the increase is hardly noticeable. It still seems that daylight comes later in the morning and darkness arrives earlier in the evening than we really like. Studies have shown a relationship between darkness and depression. Thus, light therapy has been developed to treat people whose depression is related in some way to dark, dreary days. Of course, the biblical writers often mention the importance of the light, of being in the light, of living in the light, referring to God's presence as the light that shines which no darkness can extinguish.

I suspect the most common emotional response people have to January is loneliness. The holidays are over. Parties and family gatherings have passed. Life is back to its routine. A country and western song asks the questions, "Have you ever been lonely? Have you ever been blue?" Is there anybody who has not been lonely at some time in life? I read about a high school senior who was running for class president. It was a forgone conclusion that she would win although she was neither the most attractive candidate nor the best speaker. After she won, someone asked her what the secret was to her popularity. It seemed everyone had great respect for her. She attributed her interest in people to some advice her grandmother gave her when she had said, "Ann, remember everybody is just a little bit lonely."

I read an article recently about young divorced men who live in New York City. In-depth interviews with a large number of them found them to be highly successful in business. Attractive, upwardly mobile men with enough money to afford anything they want describes them. The thing interviewers noted immediately was how "OK" they looked.

Through the interviews those asking the questions learned of the pain many of these men lived with. Dates were easy to come by. Money was no problem. But there was pain. "We never realized how much we missed someone caring for us. Someone with whom we could be comfortable, who worried if we had a cold." They went on to note how the swinging life can easily get boring and the need to be cared about by others rises to the surface. The interviewers were surprised because these men looked so good.[2]

It is an eerie, sad, uncomfortable feeling to feel lonely in a crowd, surrounded by people but making no connection. Paul Simon captured the scene and the feeling with these words from his song "The Sounds of Silence":

> And in the naked light I saw
> ten thousand people, maybe more.
> People talking without speaking,
> people hearing without listening,
> People writing songs that voices never shared,
> No one dared disturb the sounds of silence.

Often emotional pain is much more agonizing and paralyzing than physical pain. Loneliness—being by yourself when you don't want to be—is one of the most agonizing emotional pains any of us experiences.

Zacchaeus climbed the tree to get a better view. Maybe he climbed it to hide, but to hide hoping to be found. He was willing to try anything for a half-hour of companionship. Jesus found him, saw him, looked him square in the eye and said, "Zacchaeus, come on down!" And the people snickered up their sleeves because

Jesus didn't know any better than to invite himself to the house of this man Zacchaeus whom no one else would touch with a ten-foot pole.

Zacchaeus' attempt to see Jesus provides a wealth of possible descriptive titles: A Tree With a View, Out on a Limb, or Come on Down. But I really like A Short Seeker. It is descriptive of Zacchaeus and of us. Zacchaeus was hurting because he was isolated and insulated and so are we. He was short on hope, meaning, value, and purpose in life. He was seeking insight, understanding, healing. He sounds so contemporary. He sounds like us. Going at life alone isolates us. On occasions we go it alone because that is what we choose. Other times we are forced to go at life alone because others are not and will not be associated with us. It may be because of a stand we have taken, a conviction we hold, a profession we practice, a disease we have, our sexual orientation, or the color of our skin. Whenever we are isolated, regardless of the cause of the isolation, a dimension of survival instinct takes over and insulates us. We put on a mask and pretend, pretend to be happy, pretend to be enjoying life. We say that sticks and stones may break our bones, but words can never hurt us. We lie! We claim we really enjoy spending time by ourselves. That may be true when we choose whether or not to be alone. But to be isolated is to be by yourself when you do not want to be.

A few years ago an ad ran in a Kansas paper: "I will listen to you talk for thirty minutes without comment for $5.00." Does that sound like a hoax? Would anybody call? You bet! It was not long before the individual who ran the ad was receiving between ten and twenty calls a day. The pain of loneliness was so sharp that some were willing to try anything for a half-hour of companionship.

Jesus knew what Zacchaeus was saying and seeking by being up a tree, out on a limb, and he knows what we are saying and seeking when we isolate ourselves. I'm so glad Jesus said, "Zacchaeus, come on down." If he can say, "Zacchaeus, come on down," then he can say, "Howard, come on down," "Sarah, come on down," "Tom, come on down," and "Amy, come on down." Come on down from your perches of isolation, insulation, and loneliness. Come on down to relationship, to friendship, to forgiveness, to love, to grace, to acceptance.

The story is told that Michelangelo was seen rolling a huge rock down the street. He was asked what he was doing and replied, "There is an angel in here just waiting to come out." Jesus saw in Zacchaeus a peculiar treasure. The treasure was not who the world had made him; rather, the treasure was the potential he had in him to be his best. Because, of course, it was not the world that made him at all.[3]

Here is evidence that people behave differently when they are treated differently. All his professional life Zacchaeus had been treated like he had the plague or leprosy and so he was always seen on the fringes of life. People related to him only when they absolutely had to and those encounters could hardly be called relating. Along came Jesus with his open invitation, "Come on down." Suddenly, the seeker was being sought. Rather than Zacchaeus seeking Jesus, Jesus was seeking Zacchaeus. This is the way God works. Long before we ever think of seeking God, God already is seeking us. In Zacchaeus' case, not only were words exchanged over lunch, but also a life was changed.

Jesus summarized his relationship with Zacchaeus by saying, "Salvation has come to this house today . . ." (Luke 19:9). Salvation means deliverance or having enough space to get away from doing evil. Zacchaeus was lost because he was in the wrong place. That's what the word translated "lost" means. An object is lost when someone has moved it from its own place and put it in the wrong place. Zacchaeus was in the wrong place. Up a tree, out on a limb, isolated, lonely, insulated, he was in the wrong place. The place he needed to be was in relationship, relationship with God and with fellow human beings. Zacchaeus was delivered from the control of things, delivered from isolation and insulation, delivered from the rejection of others, and delivered into the love, grace, forgiveness, and acceptance of God, delivered into relationship.

Luke told this story as an illustration of what can happen to all of us sawed-off social disasters who walk around in any generation and in every generation. Our situation is different from that of Zacchaeus. We are the religious in-crowd, not the outcasts. Few, if any, of us look at Zacchaeus and see ourselves. We don't collect taxes, we pay them. We aren't short people; we stand on our soapboxes to conceal our spiritual shortness. No crowd keeps us from seeing and hearing a celebrity. We just turn on the television. We have worked hard to be respectable and we've communicated to our children that they had better not disgrace the family because what other people think about us is just about the most important thing in the world. Our camouflage is more sophisticated than sycamore leaves. We hide ourselves so well behind the faces we wear that often we don't even know who we are. We have done so many wonderful things that if we could get Jesus to eat lunch with us we would talk his ear off for about thirty seconds repeating all our grand accomplishments. Then we would be out on a limb! But Jesus would look at us, eye to eye, and say, "Come on down! You are a treasure for what you are at your best because I know who made you who you are. Come on down!" I'm so glad Jesus sought Zacchaeus. If he could seek him, he can seek me. He is seeking me. He is seeking you. Have you seen him and heard him? Are you looking and listening?

If you are not in relationship with God, then you are in the wrong place. All of us have been lonely, isolated, and insulated at times in our lives. All of us have been in the wrong place. But God comes to us, seeking and searching for us, looks at us eye to eye, regardless of what tree we've climbed or why, calls us by name, and says, "Come on down!" I am so glad Jesus said that to Zacchaeus! I'm so glad he says that to me! I'm so glad he says it to you! "Come on down!"

QUESTIONS TO PONDER

1. What causes you to feel lonely?

2. When has your job caused you to feel isolated?

3. When have people responded to you because of what you do rather than who you are?

4. What do you think Zacchaeus was seeking?

5. What do you think Jesus saw when he looked at Zacchaeus?

6. What relevance does this story about Zacchaeus and Jesus have for you?

7. Rewrite this story as your story.

10

AN AMBIVALENT SEEKER

JOHN 18:28–38

THROUGHOUT HIS MINISTRY people asked Jesus about his actions and activity. Religious leaders wondered, at first silently and later orally, why Jesus did things that were contrary to religious custom and practice. The common people, with whom Jesus was extremely popular, asked Jesus to help them, to heal them, to be a friend to them. Jesus' responses to these questions and requests increased his popularity and raised more questions.

Nearly every person who came in contact with Jesus became a seeker. There was something about Jesus' presence, the way he engaged people, the observations he made, and the questions he asked that sent people wondering, questioning, searching, and seeking. Even those who were accustomed to asking questions of others found themselves asking penetrating questions about meaning and purpose in life.

Pilate is one of the people who surprises me in this way. He's going about doing his job, and part of his job gets him involved with Jesus. Something about his interaction with Jesus begins to scratch beneath the surface and facade of Pilate's life. Pilate usually is not treated kindly in Bible study groups, sermons, or popular opinion. However, John portrays him in a more positive light. Perhaps that is because John really was striving to give theological rather than historical insights when he composed his Gospel. Seeking to learn about Pilate and his encounter with Jesus leads to exploring thoughts about God that Pilate raises rather than just his factual encounter with Jesus during the last week of Jesus' life.

Pilate is an excellent example of how encountering Christ results in asking and exploring penetrating questions about life. I encourage you to take time to read the entire section in John's Gospel related to Pilate. Notice how many questions he posed— some to the religious leaders and some to Jesus. Permit those questions to become your questions. Indeed, Pilate's questions can be the questions of a seeker. Here are Pilate's questions: What do you accuse this man of? Are you the king of the Jews? What have you done? Are you a king? What is truth? Do you want me to set free for you the king of the Jews? Where do you come from? Do you want me to crucify your king? I wonder what these questions may reveal about Pilate and about us.

Pilate was the procurator or governor of the Roman province of Judea from 26 to 36 of the Common Era. His residence normally was Caesarea but he came to Jerusalem during Passover, presumably to maintain order when the city was overcrowded with religious pilgrims. Pilate was in a politically difficult position. He surely felt the pressure from both the Roman officials and the Jewish leaders. As governor, Pilate had the responsibility of keeping order. The Jews despised the presence of Roman rule and soldiers in the land and especially in the city of Jerusalem. Their intense dislike, even hatred by some, of the Romans at least partially had to do with the Romans considering the emperor a god and often disregarding the beliefs of others. This issue had caused trouble for Pilate on an occasion when he brought soldiers into Jerusalem and had not taken the insignia of the emperor off their armaments. Previous governors had removed the insignia because of the strong stance of the Jews against graven images. Pilate had created a furor in Jerusalem a second time when he built an aqueduct through the city and used funds from the Temple treasury to help pay for it. In a sense Pilate had two strikes against him because these complaints had been registered with Rome and Rome had been sensitive to the complaints. Pilate knew the political scene well enough to know that with three strikes he was out.

In the climate of people crowding into Jerusalem for Passover, the Sanhedrin brought Jesus before Pilate. The Sanhedrin was the Jewish council made up of Saduccees and Pharisees who discussed and gave interpretations on religious matters. The fact that the Sanhedrin brought Jesus to Pilate does not mean that the Sanhedrin was unanimous in this decision. As a matter of fact, there is some evidence that Joseph of Arimathea and Nicodemus were members of the Sanhedrin. Nevertheless, Jesus was brought before Pilate and the charges against him were made.

The Jewish leaders took Jesus from the house of the high priest to the governor's palace. They didn't go inside because to enter the house of a Gentile would have made them unclean according to Jewish religious law. Pilate came outside to meet with them. He asked them what the charges were against Jesus. They simply said he had committed a crime or they would not be bothering Pilate with the matter. Pilate said, "Well, if you've already tried the man and found him guilty, then proceed with the punishment to fit the crime. Take care of it yourselves. Don't be bothering me with things you can handle yourselves."

The Jewish leaders said they were not permitted to carry out capital punishment. Since this was an occupied territory, only the Roman government could conduct capital punishment. Pilate was unclear about what was happening. The punishment did not seem to fit the crime in Pilate's mind. He went back inside to talk to Jesus. This is the first of several trips back and forth. John's account of Pilate is a classic illustration of a person caught in the middle.

When he went in to talk to Jesus, Pilate asked, "Are you the king of the Jews?" Jesus had the presence of mind to answer Pilate's question with a question. I remember hearing as a child that it was rude to respond to a question with a question, but I since have learned that responding to a question with a question is often very helpful. I also have come to realize that to answer questions with questions is a means of control and a way to get people to comply with the questioner. Jesus asked Pilate if the question he had asked were his or did someone else give him the question? Was Pilate thinking for himself and inquiring for himself or was someone else doing his thinking? Were others merely using him?

Pilate said that Jesus' own people had turned him over to him. Implied in Pilate's next question is a hint that Pilate considered the action by the Sanhedrin unusual. He asked Jesus, "What have you done?" Pilate knew what charges had been brought against Jesus. He asked his question to find out if Jesus knew what the charges were, to get a confession out of Jesus, or to get Jesus' side of the story. The wording of the question plus additional information given by John suggests that Pilate was suspicious of the charges and thus was suspicious that he was being used by many of the Jewish religious leaders.

Jesus' response troubled Pilate. The more he talked with Jesus, the more difficulty Pilate had understanding why Jesus was such a threat to some of the religious leaders. The more Pilate talked with Jesus, the more puzzled he became about Jesus. Even though Pilate had heard the charges brought against Jesus, it is as if he thought there must be more to all of this uproar than what he had been told. So, Pilate asked Jesus, "What have you done?"

Jesus responded to Pilate's question about what he had done in a way that was difficult for Pilate to comprehend. Jesus said his kingdom was not of this world, that it did not function in the same manner that a political kingdom usually functioned. Jesus' illustration of this was that when he was handed over to the Jewish authorities, his followers did not fight to keep him from being taken. Of course Peter had attempted to do that and Jesus had reprimanded him immediately. This suggests that even those closest and most involved with Jesus had difficulty comprehending *kingdom* as he used and defined the term.

Pilate continued the dialogue with another variation on the same question. "Are you a king, then?" When the other Gospel writers recorded this question, the response they wrote as Jesus' answer was, "So you say." How frustrated Pilate must have been! No doubt he wanted Jesus just to answer the question with a simple yes or no. I was asked to be a character witness in a divorce case by one party and then subpoenaed by the other party to appear in court in the case. The attorney began with questions to which he wanted yes or no answers, but either answer I would have given would have revealed confidential information. I refused to answer the question on three occasions. Each time the judge interpreted for the attorney the uniqueness of my position. I sensed that the lawyer became more and more frustrated because he could get neither a yes nor a no answer to his questions. I sense that Pilate felt that type of frustration when he asked Jesus if he were king of the Jews and Jesus responded, "So you say." In other words Jesus said, "This is your way of saying who I am, but it is not my way." Jesus chose not to refer to himself as king of the Jews because what he meant by that and what others interpreted it to mean were radically different. Meaning is adequately conveyed only when a listener hears what the speaker intends.

The term *king* was a volatile word during Jesus' day. For the Israelites it meant deliverer, and they expected a military leader. For the Romans it meant a competitor for the emperor, an insurrectionist, one who was seeking to usurp the power and authority of Caesar. They may have claimed Jesus said he was king of the Judeans rather than king of the Jews. That might have been even more troublesome to Pilate because he was the ruler for Rome over the territory of Judea.

Jesus' meaning of the term *king* was different from the views of either the Jewish leaders or Pilate. Jesus saw himself as deliverer but not with force or coercion. The deliverance Jesus offered was tied up with the power of truth. On another occasion Jesus had spoken of the liberating power of truth. Jesus defined his purpose in the world as speaking about the truth and stated that those who belong to the truth listened to him.

This climactic confession of Jesus represents a significant testimony of the unity of power and truth. Most civilizations have been built on the assumption that the two are incompatible, that power is irrational and that truth is impotent. The tensions are well known. Against this disastrous alienation Jesus affirmed both that he who witnesses to the truth exercises a power that will prevail and, conversely, that he who would reign must submit his power to the test of truth. Pilate had been schooled to believe that kings ruled by might and not by truth, that truth was on the side of the biggest battalions. Looking at this young Jewish "king" in fetters before him he was moved to ask, "What is truth?" Little could he dream that when his Caesar had been long forgotten, this man's truth would reign over a vaster domain than Rome had ever known.

Pilate may be the best known person who asked the question "What is truth?" but there are ways and times when each person asks that question. Asking the question is the beginning of acknowledgment. Asking the question is the first step to knowing what it does, and to have it engulf the one who is raising the question. The truth, at its least, in the context in which Pilate asked the question is that the kingdom over which Christ reigns is in the world but not of the world. It is the kingdom that goes to the very heart of life and deals with the motives and motivations of life. It is a kingdom that rules the wills of people. It is a kingdom that seeks peace and truth. The irony is that a person cannot have one without the other. To be at peace is to know the truth. To know the truth is to be at peace.

If there was ever anyone who was depicted as anxious and not at peace, it was Pilate. Pilate came in and went out. He stood up. He sat down. He asked questions and he had questions asked of him. It was a hand-wringing experience for him and eventually he thought that if he washed his hands maybe he would feel better, relieved, as if he were rid of the responsibility. But that did not work either (though Pilate did leave the legacy of a double meaning for washing one's hands of something).

Pilate's apparent conclusion was that Jesus was innocent. Yet he seemed unwilling to act on his own evidence and intuition. When the Sanhedrin met in the early dawn hours, they charged Jesus with blasphemy, which means insulting God. They knew that charge would get them nowhere with Pilate. So they levied these three charges against Jesus when they came before Pilate: 1) Jesus was a revolutionary, 2) he was urging people not to pay their taxes, and 3) he was claiming to be a king. Luke's Gospel tells that Pilate sent Jesus to Herod since Jesus was a Galilean. Herod sent him back to Pilate, an indication that Herod found him innocent. Thus, Luke suggests that two male witnesses, Pilate and Herod, testified to Jesus' innocence. According to Jewish law, when two witnesses agreed, their decision was to be accepted. But it was not so in this situation. Jesus had infuriated the religious leadership to such a degree that they were not going to let him get away.

By now, Pilate is convinced of Jesus' innocence. He seems to think the religious leaders will be satisfied with his decision. After all he is the governor. Yet Pilate does not use the authority he has and declare Jesus innocent. Rather, in his desire to keep the crowd at bay, to keep them from turning on him, he asked if they wouldn't really like to have this Jesus set free. It was his custom each Passover to release a prisoner. I wonder if this were a way to appease the Jews who often felt that innocent fellow Jews were arrested and detained on unreasonable charges for unreasonable lengths of time. According to Matthew, Pilate asked which Jesus they wanted released, Jesus Barabbas, whose name meant Jesus the son of a father, or Jesus the Messiah, the anointed one of God. Jesus Barabbas was a known bandit and thug who had robbed and probably would rob again. Jesus the Messiah had not violated any person. But the religious leaders preferred releasing someone who might rob from them and maybe kill one of them rather then release someone whom they felt threatened their authority and position in life.

Then Pilate had Jesus beaten and mocked as a leader. And he paraded him out in front of the religious leaders. Perhaps he thought that if he humiliated and ridiculed Jesus, the leaders would be satisfied. But their anger and fear and hatred of Jesus had become so intense that they would not be satisfied with anything less than Jesus' death.

All of this so troubled Pilate that he went back to Jesus and said, "Where do you come from?" I think this was a question of exasperation. Pilate was asking in essence, "Who in the world are you? What have you done that has so stirred up these people that they will be satisfied with nothing less than your death?"

Although this was Jesus' trial, it was very trying on Pilate. There is indication in each of the Gospel accounts that Jesus remained silent when asked about the charges against him. Who can keep silent for any length of time, especially when we are anxious or nervous? Are there not times when we feel compelled to say something even when we have nothing to say? Why didn't Jesus say something when the false charges were brought against him? Even now Jesus' silence continues to be frustrating. It was frustrating to Pilate, and twenty centuries later we are asking basically the same question, "Why didn't you say something, Jesus?" It is amazing how powerful silence can be and how powerless one can feel in the face of it. Jesus was aware that nothing he would or could say would silence his accusers. Their minds were made up. Probably any statement he made only would have fueled more hostility. For three years Jesus had been saying things, many of which were confrontational to the religious leaders. They were so angered by what Jesus had been saying that they would not listen to what he said. This happens all the time. We become so angered or agitated by someone that we refuse to hear what he or she are saying. The truth will make them mad before it sets them free.

Pilate was convinced of Jesus' innocence, but he was unwilling to release him. His reasons must be tied up with his concern for his job and the importance of crowd control. Later legend in Christianity was very sympathetic to Pilate and tended to blame the death of Jesus on the Jews and exonerate Pilate completely. Over the years, many in Christianity have based anti-Semitic words and actions on this bias. In fact, only a few of the Jews were responsible for Jesus' death—certain members of the religious establishment. Jesus had tried to reform Judaism and reformers are usually met with resistance, even outright, overt hostility. Many Jews were followers of Jesus. Not only was Jesus born a Jew but remained a Jew all of his life. There is no indication that he intended or wanted to start a new religious group or organization.

Indeed, Pilate, a Gentile and a Roman governor, contributed to the death of Jesus. He could have kept it from happening but did not. Legend has come to say that Pilate's wife, who was said to have been a Jewish proselyte and was called Claudia Porcula, became a Christian. It was held that even Pilate himself became a Christian. Today the Coptic Church ranks Pilate and his wife as saints and honors them on June 25th. Pilate was warned by the dream of his wife, by his conscience, and by his sense of justice that Jesus was innocent, but he decided to appease the crowd. Maybe later Pilate recognized his indecision for what it was and came around.

Certainly, from the material available to us in the Gospels, when Pilate was in the presence of Christ, he became a seeker. Jesus' presence and interaction with Pilate raised many concerns for Pilate and caused him to ask question after question. How did Pilate resolve these questions? From what the biblical writers tell us, he didn't. He is classically indecisive. Maybe later he saw the futility of his indecision, that not to decide is to decide. Pilate was a seeker. However, the biblical material gives no indication that he resolved his seeking by accepting God's love and grace. Maybe he did later. Maybe he didn't. I'm undecided.

Pilate's anxiety is shown by his questions. What he asked and when he raised his questions suggest how uneasy Pilate was. The last question that Pilate asked according to John's Gospel shows clearly Pilate's exasperation and the religious leaders' desperation. Pilate asked, "Do you want me to crucify your king?" By this time Pilate seems to have lost all ability to think and act for himself. He had given his mind and his actions over to the crowd as if he had become a puppet on a string. He would respond according to the string that the crowd pulled. In essence Pilate said, "Tell me what you want me to do and I will do it. I will do anything to get out of this situation without an uproar and a riot." Thus he asked, "Do you want me to crucify your king?"

Notice the response that John wrote the chief priests made, "The only king we have is the Emperor!" How incriminating! They who on other occasions had taught, urged, and argued that God was their king and to acknowledge anyone else as king was blasphemous and idolatrous, now had come full circle and were willing to say and do anything to get rid of the person who was a threat to their view and way of life. It is an old and often repeated story. It is as old as Scripture and repeated today when people in any land equate the action of their government with the action of God.

Pilate played "Twenty Questions" with Jesus primarily as a defense mechanism, which he thought would get him out of a difficult situation. Hints between the lines suggest that Pilate anticipated that the people would allow him to question Jesus, scourge Jesus, and then let him go. When Pilate's plan did not go as he expected, he became anxious. His anxiety increased as he asked questions and received unexpected answers or no answers.

Was Jesus king of the Jews? Was Jesus a king? Not in the way the term is typically used. Jesus' invitation to discipleship is a call for radical reformation in our lives. Too many of us do not want to change as much as Jesus suggested with his words and his living.

We claim someone else as king in our lives and crucify afresh this Son of God whose presence in our midst continues to raise questions—difficult, mind-stretching, disturbing questions that require struggle, agony, and turning around in our lives for us to answer them. Too many of us would rather continue going in the wrong direction than to invest the time and energy that changing directions would involve. We, like Pilate, play "Twenty Questions" as a means to avoid facing who we are and who God wants us to be.

We are so much like Pilate. We look in the face of some crowd and ask, "What do you want me to do?" What we need to do is to look into the face of God and ask God, "What do you want me to do?" This is the seeker's true question. I don't know if Pilate ever asked God this question. But you can. Will you?

QUESTIONS TO PONDER

1. In what ways do you understand Pilate to be a seeker?
2. What is most promising about Pilate?
3. What is most pathetic about Pilate?
4. What parallels are there between you and Pilate?
5. What are your "Twenty Questions"?
6. Do your questions reveal that you are a seeker?
7. For what are you seeking?

11

A Q U E S T I O N I N G   S E E K E R

JOHN 20:19–31

As CHRISTIANITY DEVELOPED there came to be seasons that the Church celebrated: Advent, Christmas, Epiphany, Lent, Easter, and Pentecost. The Sunday following Easter became known as Low Sunday. Originally, the designation of Low Sunday was all emotional, but it later came to have a numerical meaning. If you attend worship on Easter and the following Sunday, then you are well aware of the numerical contrast in attendance between Easter Sunday and Low Sunday. For the original disciples, the way John tells the story, both Easter Sunday and the following Sunday were low Sundays emotionally. The disciples gathered somewhere in a room behind closed doors; some versions of the Bible translate the word "locked" doors. They were cloistered in a room, lying low. They were locked in fear, frightened that what some of the Jewish religious leaders and the Romans had done to Jesus would be done to them. Fear will make people lie low. And that would certainly make for a low Sunday.

I wonder how you are lying low. Are you involved in a congregation? Is the congregation lying low in fear of some issue(s)? What issues are being avoided? The issues we seek to avoid may serve as excellent hints of how and when we as individuals lie low and when the organization of which we are a part lies low. I wonder what would happen if we permitted the love and grace of God to raise us up out of the deadness of lying low. We might be surprised at what would happen.

A significant event transpired on the first Low Sunday that invites our examination—the reaction of Thomas to the news that Jesus had been raised from the dead and his ensuing responses. I recommend Thomas as our teacher and invite you to join me in exploring his life to learn about our relationships with God and ourselves. Thomas, for me, is the patron saint of late believers.

What do you know about Thomas? What we do know about Thomas we owe to John's Gospel. Actually, we don't even know his name. He is known by a characteristic. He was a twin. That is what Thomas means in Aramaic, and so he is identified simply as the Twin. He is listed in the middle of the twelve in all four Gospels. Whether that means he always was in the middle of things or that he was neither the stronger nor the weaker of the twelve, there is no way to discern.

His interactions with others give some clue of what Thomas was like. When Jesus set his face toward Jerusalem, all of the disciples attempted to dissuade him from going into the lion's den in Jerusalem—all, that is, except Thomas. It was Thomas who said, "Let us go along with the Teacher, so that we may die with him!" (John 11:16) Does that statement express sad resignation or loyal commitment? Since we do not have a recording of Thomas' voice, we cannot discern his inflection and emphasis. If he was expressing loyal commitment, he later abandoned his loyalty, because he, like the rest, scattered in the face of Jesus' execution.

At the last meal Jesus ate with his disciples he said that he was going away and that they knew the way to go where he was going. Well, maybe the rest of them knew the way but Thomas didn't and he was willing to admit it. He even admitted he didn't have the foggiest idea where Jesus was going, much less how to get there.

Thomas was a person of honesty. Thomas raised tough questions, the kind that made everyone else nervous because no one knew the answers but none of the others thought you ought to admit you did not know the answers. Thomas refused to silence the integrity of his mind. Faith and reason would be joined for Thomas or he would know the reasons why not. This type of integrity is essential for emotional, mental, physical, and spiritual health. There are plenty of folks around who clearly indicate that when it comes to matters religious, don't think, just believe. Thomas was one who said that faith was a matter of both the heart and the head. Failure to integrate faith and reason was a breech of integrity for Thomas.

Boris Pasternak wrote in *Doctor Zhivago:*

> Your health is bound to be affected if, day after day, you say the opposite of what you feel, if you grovel before what you dislike and rejoice at what brings nothing but misfortune. Our nervous system isn't just a fiction; it's a part of our physical body, and our soul exists in space, and is inside us, like the teeth in our mouth. It can't be forever violated with impunity.[1]

It is a sad picture when one is dishonest with oneself and others by struggling to separate faith and reason, to turn on the heart at the expense of turning off the mind—seeking to please others by saying what one does not believe and by acting on that about which one is not convicted. Health is ruined—physically and spiritually. Thomas refused to take that path because he was a person of honesty.

Thomas was also a person of doubt. He was a realist. His world left no room for resurrection. When a person was dead, he was dead. He had seen Jesus die, and hearsay comments and secondhand faith could not form an adequate foundation for his belief. In the midst of his doubt Thomas did not put down the belief of others or attempt to force his doubts onto them. When the disciples told Thomas that Christ was alive, he did not say, "You're crazy. Surely you don't really believe that." Neither did he say, "I'll never believe such a tale as that." Rather Thomas responded, "I won't believe this story until I have had firsthand experience by seeing the scars and putting my finger in those scarred hands and putting my hand in that wounded side."

Thomas was not present when Jesus appeared to his disciples after the resurrection. We tend to berate Thomas for being absent. We berate him because there have been times when we have been late or absent and missed something important. We berate Thomas because he represents all those people we think should in church but are elsewhere. We berate him because he initially refused to believe in the resurrection. Incredible! Why wouldn't he believe what the others told him? But he was no different than the other ten apostles. When the women told them, they thought what the women said was nonsense (Luke 24:11). Why don't we berate the other ten? Whatever Thomas' reason for going to Jerusalem with Jesus, even if he intended to be willing to die with Jesus, he backed away somewhere along the way with the others. The Gospel records reveal that all of the followers of Jesus except three or four of the women and "the disciple whom [Jesus] loved" (John 19:26) fled the scene of Jesus' crucifixion.

Thomas' experience and his integrity are incentives for us. No person's faith can rest on another person's experience. We benefit from knowing about the journeys of others and what routes they have taken in their development of faith. We appreciate and are strengthened by comparisons and contrasts, by similarities and by experiences completely foreign to us. But we cannot adopt someone else's faith. People have to move beyond the faith of their parents, teachers, and friends to a faith that is theirs. Otherwise all they have is hand-me-down religion, and hand-me-down religion won't survive the first serious crisis it faces. Secondhand religion has little, if any, genuine faith in it, because it just accepts what is handed down without question. Secondhand religion doesn't usually survive the first serious grief, the first major temptation, or the first year of college. Some don't have much religion to lose and what some have isn't worth keeping because it really is not theirs. Thomas clearly demonstrates a seeker looking, needing, wanting firsthand faith.

There is no way to know if Thomas was still fleeing, was hiding all by himself, or had completely recovered from the shock of it all by Easter. Maybe Thomas was off by himself trying to make some sense out of life now that this greatest tragedy had jolted him. Perhaps the tragedy of Jesus' death was more trauma than Thomas could handle in the presence of others. Maybe he was off having a cup of coffee or sitting in the park feeding the pigeons. Maybe he was visiting the sick and imprisoned, clothing the naked and feeding the hungry. There is no way to know where Thomas was. All John tells us is where Thomas was not. What John tells us is that the disciples, whether the inner circle of ten or perhaps others as well, gathered on the evening of the first Easter, but Thomas was not there.

At some point, later in the evening or one day during the week some of the disciples saw Thomas and reported to him, "We have seen the Lord!" Here is where we catch a glimpse of Thomas' integrity. Thomas did not believe the testimony of his fellow disciples and he had the integrity to tell them he did not believe. It was Thomas' own way of saying that at that point in time he did not believe in God or at least not in God as he had been believing.

What about you? Have there ever been times in your life when you did not believe in God? Have you ever been willing to say that you didn't believe in God? Or have you given in to fear and said things you did not believe? Several years ago a person confessed in my office, "I believe but I don't." Maybe those words give expression to where you have been or currently are as you think about God in the context of your living. If so, I want you to meet your brother in the faith, or should I say unfaith, Thomas.

George Buttrick wrote that belief in God is natural.[2] Everyone believes in God at some time. Children take to faith in God as birds to the air. Doubts come at adolescence, but there could not be doubt except where there is first faith; and even then the young mind dimly understands what doubt is—the shadow cast by faith.

There are those who are confirmed atheists. Others of us belong to the society of Thomas; we are periodic atheists. Even the use of the word *atheist* is a negative of the term *theist*, which means believer in God. Thus, Buttrick is right. Not to believe in God is based on the concept that the unbeliever once believed in God. I don't know what percentage of people at any given moment don't believe in God. I don't know how many of those who read this don't believe in God. I don't know how many readers have their doubts about God. However, I do know some of the major bases for unbelief. There are those who see belief in God as nothing more than an objectification of purely human ideals, wishes, longings, or needs. In other words, God is seen as the perfect human being, were one to exist. Thus, the atheist sees this kind of God as only a figment of people's imaginations. A second basis for rejecting belief in God is because such faith is somehow inconsistent with the scientific method and view of reality. Theology and the church have historically opposed free scientific research and hindered the pursuit of truth for its own sake. Many within Christianity have been suspicious of inquiries that might upset the supposedly revealed truths of the Church. Copernicus, Galileo, and Darwin have been opposed and denounced by many within the Church. Such attitudes cause Arnulf Overland to conclude that the believer is not supposed to think, just believe!

Some do not believe in God because *God* is an ambiguous term whose meaning cannot be clearly communicated. Others struggle with the existence of God in the face of human suffering. A six-year-old girl returning from Sunday school frames the question, "Why are little girls in Africa starving while I have plenty to eat? Doesn't God love them as much as he does me?"

Many arrive at unbelief after observing that some of the most ardent and vocal believers are the least concerned about the injustice around them and often are seen heading the charge against social change. There are multitudes of people, including many who are seriously committed to the highest human values, who have no personal awareness of God. Thus, the argument has merit that often unbelievers in God do more for the good of others than do believers.

Occasionally, someone says to me, "I don't believe in God." I usually respond, "Tell me about the God in whom you don't believe." Permit me to tell you about the God in whom I do not believe. I do not believe in a God who is waiting to catch us in sin and punish us unmercifully. I do not believe in a God who causes disease and destruction that result in suffering and agony for an individual, a family, a group of families, or a segment of the world's population. I do not believe in a God who instructs one nation to go to war against another nation. I do not believe in a God who instructs one individual to harm another. I do not believe in a God who instructs a group or nation to pound another group or nation into oblivion. I do not believe in a God who wreaks havoc in people's live, sends disease, trouble, problems, and destruction to teach people lessons. I do not believe in a God who favors people because they happen to live in a certain country. I do not believe in a God who says that thinking and believing are incompatible. I do not believe in a God who asks us to develop less than our total selves as persons. I confess there are times when I sit in my study thinking of you and wondering about what is happening in many of your lives, wondering what I can say to you, and trying to get a handle on who and what God is, and at times I find it difficult to believe in God. I do not believe in a God who becomes angry, disgusted, and rejecting of me because at times I do not believe in God.

If you have similar struggles, then you and I are in good company. We have a brother in Thomas. There was a time when Thomas did not believe in God and he had the integrity to admit it. It is important to notice that in his not believing in God, Thomas was still accepted by his fellow disciples and included in the group.

A second observation about Thomas is his refusal to accept secondhand or hand-me-down religion. You have heard someone say or maybe you have said it yourself in a difficult, trying situation, "It just about made me lose my religion." Many do lose their religion, at least for periods during their lives. Traditional religion, what has been handed down from one generation to another, won't survive the first serious test it faces. It is hand-me-down religion. It may look good, sound good, and feel good, but it won't quite fit. It may be mama's religion, Sunday school religion, someone else's religion, unexamined religion. As L. D. Johnson described it, "It is like a cut flower which wilts and shatters. It has no way of renewing itself, and lasts only as long as it is refrigerated away from the challenging atmosphere of everyday life."[3]

Some people do not have much religion to lose. And some religion ought to be lost. It isn't worth keeping. So it was for Thomas. He lost what he had believed. The great experiment had run out. Thomas' integrity would not permit him to deal with the resurrected Lord secondhand. He said, "Unless I see the scars of the nails in his hands and put my finger on those scars and my hand in his side, I will not believe."

Secondhand belief was insufficient, inadequate, actually worse than no faith for Thomas. Thomas' atheism stripped away his secondhand faith, his preconceived notions of what God was like and how God ought to act. His moorings had come loose and life was tenuous, insecure, but Thomas refused to say he believed when he did not. How comfortable he would have been to say he believed! How much he wanted to convince himself he believed! His ten friends believed. Surely all of them could not be wrong. Even though Thomas did not believe the resurrection, even though he categorically said, "I do not believe," he was accepted in the fellowship and friendship of the disciples. I wonder if we can be that inclusive of those who honestly say, "I do not believe."

Martin Buber is credited with saying that the atheist staring from his attic window is often nearer to God than the believer caught up in his own false image of God. To listen attentively to the criticisms of honest and serious atheists can be for believers a new learning experience and one that may open the way to a deeper and truer understanding of and relationship with God. There is more faith in honest doubt than in all the creeds. And as another has noted, "Doubt is the mother of faith." Paul Schilling speaks for me, saying that the serious atheist who wrestles with ultimate questions is likely to contribute more to intelligent understanding of both God and people than the pious believer who placidly accepts prevailing views.

Is not Thomas a witness to the truth of this statement? What if he had placidly accepted the prevailing view of his colleagues and comrades? Thomas was flatly and openly incredulous, pushing the whole appearance thing aside as being ridiculously impossible. Thomas had a doggedly honest mind. There is not much poetry in Thomas. He was a matter-of-fact person—not one to be rushed into believing what he wanted to believe, but sincere enough to face the facts and to accept them, however grim and dark. Thomas did not still his unbelief by pretending it did not exist. When is unbelief ever stilled by pretension?

We are insensitive, unthinking, and uncaring when we do not make room in our fellowship for unbelievers, for atheists. Harry Emerson Fosdick said it well, "Through a long lifetime I have watched this endlessly repeated tragedy: defenders of the faith presenting the faith in indefensible terms and alienating the minds they might have won."[4] The struggle through unbelief to belief leads to firsthand encounters with Christ and can cause one to exclaim with Thomas, "My Lord and my God!"

It was another Thomas, Thomas Carlyle, who said that every parish needs a person who knows God as more than secondhand. Only when the gospel of Christ is firsthand evidence, something that has happened to us—only then does our belief grow vital.

Thomas' experience demonstrates for us the difference between comfortable religion and comforting faith. Comfortable religion seduces us. It tells us to eat, drink, and be merry. It urges us to accept the status quo. Comfortable religion coaxes us to stay the course. Comfortable religion says don't go where you don't know what is there. Comfortable religion tells us not to examine or think about things that are disturbing or upsetting. Comfortable religion says shrink back from life. Comfortable religion says build a wall around your life and withdraw from the world. Comforting faith, however, challenges us to stretch our minds. Comforting faith encourages us to believe in the possibilities we have not yet realized. Comforting faith equips us to deal with the unknown, to go out not knowing where we are going but confident of the Presence that is wherever we go. Comforting faith enables us to deal with life and the world with hope and promise. Comforting faith says build bridges in your life, be in the world but not of the world.

The Bible is intended to produce in us the kind of faith that emerged from Thomas. This kind of faith begins with honesty. Everything is on the table. Faith and reason learn to work together. No questions are dodged, no convictions silenced. If doubts arise, so be it. Doubt can be beneficial.

You may have come to genuine, firsthand faith in the resurrected Christ in another way. Great! Celebrate! Maybe Mary Magdalene or Peter or some other is the model for you. But for me Thomas is a fellow struggler, pilgrim, brother in the faith, and patron saint of late believers.

If you still need to come to faith in the risen Lord, don't quit, don't give up, don't stop seeking. You may have doubts, questions, unbelief. Maybe you are struggling with reconciling faith and reason. I commend Thomas to you.

The journey from unbelief to belief in God often is a long, difficult trip. Thomas is a model for us of how the road is traveled. Notice what happened to Thomas. He did not believe and said he did not believe. Jesus broke in upon him and said by his presence that whatever Thomas had done, whatever he had been, whatever he had believed or not believed, Jesus still trusted Thomas and believed in him. God believes in us when we don't believe in ourselves and when we don't believe in God. Only when we confess our unbelief is there any hope for us to come to terms with it. Only then can we journey from unbelief to belief, from hand-me-down religion to firsthand religion, from comfortable religion to comforting faith. Then, we will discover that like Thomas we are being fashioned into new types of beings, we are becoming new creatures, living in a new world, endowed by Christ with new possibilities and powers.

"This," says John as he lays down his pen, "is what I have written in my book to prove what Christ can do for anyone who will accept it from him." May it be so in your life as it was in the life of Thomas. From the way John told the story, Thomas was the last of the disciples to come to belief in the resurrected Lord. Thomas came late to his faith in God. Indeed, Thomas is the patron saint of the late believers. Perhaps nowhere does the cliché "Better late than never" have more relevance. I commend Thomas to you. Learn from him.

QUESTIONS TO PONDER

1. What is your opinion of Thomas?

2. What evidence is there that Thomas was seeking God?

3. What are your thoughts about Thomas being accepted by believers although he clearly stated that he did not believe?

4. What events or circumstances have contributed to your unbelief, to your not believing in God?

5. Describe the god in whom you do not believe.

6. What is most frightening to you about Thomas or about what I have written about him?

7. What is more reassuring about Thomas for you?

12

A SEEKING BUSINESSWOMAN

ACTS 16:11–40

DO YOU REALIZE the variety of filters we use daily? When I make coffee I use a filter so the coffee grounds don't flow into the pot of freshly brewed coffee. Filters are essential in the air conditioning and heating units of our homes to remove dust from the air. It is amazing how much dust is filtered through the heating and cooling systems in homes we thought we were keeping clean. Photographers use filters on camera lenses to assist with the clarity and effect they want to create in pictures. All of us use mental filters as we think about what we want to tell someone. Mentally we are processing what we will say and won't say as well as how we will express ourselves.

Are you aware of the filters that cover your eyes and ears? Do you see people who are unkempt and seek to keep your distance from them? Do you see men with long hair and/or beards and make negative judgments about them? Do you hear people speaking in a language you do not understand and wonder what they are doing here? Do you hear people speak with a southern accent and feel drawn to them immediately? Do you distance yourself from someone who speaks with a Bronx accent? Right now you are filtering what you reading. You may be using the filter of cynicism or pain or delight. And I filtered this material thinking of you as I was writing. We use all types of filters as we see, hear, and interact with people.

We also use a variety of filters when we explore and study the Scriptures. We often overlay Scripture with the filter of culture as well as the filters of our ethical, moral, or political agenda. There was a time when some people who believed in slavery used passages of Scripture about slaves to support slavery. There are those today who feel strongly that women should only be in maternal roles. They will use passages of Scripture to support their positions. When we use these and other filters to read and hear Scripture, we fail to read and hear the whole message of Scripture.

Through this book I am exploring events in the lives of several individuals who I sense were seeking to encounter God in a way that would enhance their lives and contribute more meaning to their lives. In this chapter I focus on Lydia. Not a great deal of information is known about Lydia, but what we know portrays a woman quite different from what people often think and understand women to have been like in the first century of the Common Era.

Lydia was from Thyatira, a city in Lydia. Lydia may have gotten her name from her homeland. She may have been Sarah or Mary of Lydia, but in meeting, interacting with people, and people telling about her, Lydia became a nickname by which she was known. If we trace the family histories of many Smiths in this country, we learn that their ancestors worked as silversmiths, goldsmiths, and blacksmiths. John the silversmith became known as John Smith. Something similar probably happened to Lydia.

The country of Lydia was in southwest Asia Minor. Although it was a coastal country, its strength lay inland. Sardis was its capital. The Greeks influenced the art and styles of the Lydians and Persians. During Roman times, there were well-known guilds of woolworkers and dyers in Lydia. Perfumes were sold in containers of an elegant shape that were known as Lydion.

There were ancient religious cults in Lydia. From the time of Antiochus III, around 223 B.C.E., there was also a significant Jewish influence in Lydia. Sometime during or after the Babylonian exile, approximately 2,000 Jewish families were settled in Lydia and

Phrygia. Both Sardis and Thyatira in Lydia had Jewish communities during the Roman times. The rise of Christianity in Lydia is evident in that three of the churches to which letters are written in the book of Revelation are in Lydia: Sardis, Thyatira, and Philadelphia.

Lydia is mentioned only in the sixteenth chapter of Acts. Were it not for Luke, we would not know about Lydia as a seeker who became a significant person in the development of followers of Christ in the town of Philippi.

Luke was on a journey with Paul and Silas. They sailed from Troas to Samothrace and then to Neopolis. From Neopolis they traveled inland to Philippi, a Roman colony. A Roman colony was a little bit of Rome planted in a foreign land. It was an outpost where Roman soldiers and officials would be sent. There was some natural interaction between the Romans and citizens of the community.

In Philippi was a businesswoman from Thyatira whose name was Lydia. She owned a cloth shop. She sold only purple cloth. Talk about specialization! Why would anyone sell only purple cloth? How could she possibly make a living selling only one color of cloth? When I go to buy cloth, I want to see bolts and bolts of cloth with every color, shade, and hue of the rainbow represented so I can choose exactly the correct color. Why did Lydia sell only one color of cloth?

Lydia did not use good marketing techniques at all. One marketing class in a major university and Lydia could have revolutionized the textile industry. If she had taken a survey or just asked a few people on the streets of Philippi, she would have learned that her sales would have increased tremendously if she had offered even two colors of cloth. But one color and purple at that? Who would buy purple cloth? Maybe I should. People often comment about a suit or sport coat I wear. Maybe I should have a purple suit in honor of Lydia.

Of course, we have been spoiled. A computer program called CorelDRAW has more than 400 colors from which to choose. What a selection of color choices! With the developments in the textile industry through the years, the options and choices for us seem limitless. Several years ago I met a person whose expertise is bleaching denim. His work was to help his company make new jeans look faded, pale, worn. What specialization!

Lydia was at the other end of the textile industry. She was self-employed, operating her cloth shop in Philippi. She sold one color of cloth, purple. Lydia's cloth was expensive. Her native land of Lydia was on the seacoast. There was a certain shellfish that produced a secretion that was used as dye. This dye was purple in color and had to be gathered drop by drop from the shellfish. A pound of wool dyed with this purple dye cost about $60 in 50 C.E. That was a lot of money in those days. Purple was the color of royalty. It was the color of wealth. Frankly, it was about the only color available in those days. Apparently, Lydia was fairly high on the socioeconomic scale of her day. A considerable amount of capital would have been needed to purchase wool dyed purple in the country of Lydia and have it transported to Philippi where the woman Lydia was in business.

Apparently Paul and his entourage arrived in Philippi early in the week. Luke indicates they spent several days in town before the Sabbath. On the Sabbath they looked for Old First Synagogue of Philippi where they could worship, but there was no synagogue in the town. Why not?

Wherever Jewish settlers gathered, synagogues were developed if there were ten Jewish men in the community. The practical reason for this was that it took ten households to provide and maintain the ministry of a synagogue and to provide the critical mass of people to have a congregation. There were emotional and spiritual roots to the number ten as well. The minimum number required to share the Passover meal was ten. In towns where there were not ten Jewish men to form a synagogue, there would be a place designated where the Jews would meet for prayer, often by the riverside, perhaps as a reminder of the Exodus and the crossing of the Reed Sea, which was like a river. Apparently there were not enough Jewish men in Philippi to form a synagogue. However, the word for *prayer* used by Greek-speaking Jews was a synonym for synagogue. Perhaps Luke's comment that some women were gathering for prayer is a suggestion that a synagogue was formed where people gathered for prayer, whether or not there was an official location or building.

Lydia was faithful in her relationship with God. Luke identifies her as "a worshiper of God." Being a native of Thyatira, which had a Jewish community that settled there during or after the Babylonian exile, Lydia could have been from a Jewish family. Or Lydia may have been a Gentile convert to Judaism. Whatever path her faith development had taken, in Philippi where Paul met her, Lydia was one of the women gathering down by the riverside to pray.

Luke skips hurriedly on in telling the story of Paul's encounter with Lydia. We have such a minuscule amount of information about an event that led to a major contribution, impact, and witness for the followers of Christ. Referring to Lydia, Luke wrote, "She was a woman who worshiped God, and the Lord opened her mind to pay attention to what Paul was saying." Clearly, Luke is making the point that Lydia's decision to become a follower of the Way was the work of God and not due to Paul's skill.

Early followers of Christ were identified as followers of the Way of Christ. This reference suggested that Christ's followers were on a lifelong pilgrimage. Later the reference was abbreviated and the shorthand version, the Way, became a well-known identification of the early disciples of Christ.

Lydia was intrigued by what Paul had to say. Obviously, she was a seeker. She was a person open to encounters with God. She, like many others, discovered that encounters with God often come in, through, and as result of encounters with people. The fact that Lydia was a worshiper of God who regularly went down by the riverside to pray with others tells us she continually put herself in a place and availed herself of the opportunity to encounter God. She was continually seeking God, drawing from God, being addressed by God.

One of the earliest external faith expressions used by followers of the Way was baptism. Luke says that Lydia paid attention to what Paul was saying. And then she and those who were part of her household were baptized. God opened Lydia's life to the good news and she in response immediately opened her home in hospitality. Hospitality is one of the oldest and most important traits of the followers of Christ. In a sense, Lydia really put Paul on the spot. She said, "Come and stay in my house if you have decided that I am a true believer in the Lord." What could Paul do other than stay at her house? Having talked with Lydia and having participated in some way in her baptism, how could Paul suggest that she was not a true believer?

In his letter to the Philippians, we discover that the church at Philippi was the one with which Paul had the strongest, deepest love and joy. Although Paul never mentions Lydia in his letter to the Philippians, it was her hospitality that relieved Paul of the necessity of earning a living while he was in Philippi working with the congregation there. Paul also accepted gifts from the church at Philippi while he was working with other churches. Paul had a special love for the church at Philippi. I'm convinced that Lydia was the chief cause of this unique relationship because in seeking God her life was opened to the good news and she in turn opened her home in hospitality to fellow seekers of the Way.

By telling us about Lydia and her seeking, Luke tells us a great deal about the early church. In this brief story, we are told that followers of the Way did things differently than was the custom or according to culture or accepted tradition. Paul and Silas were Near-Eastern males talking to women in public. That was different. Twice in Luke's Gospel, Luke mentions women who followed Jesus from Galilee (Luke 23:49, 55). Luke shows interest in "those of low degree." Women are the first evangelists, announcers of good news, who ran to tell the male disciples (who were hiding) that Jesus had risen from the dead (Luke 24:9). The early church seemed radical in the way it welcomed women and featured them as leaders and prophets in the context of conventional Jewish and Greco-Roman ideas about women. Women could be members of this movement without the permission of their husbands and could initiate divorce from a pagan husband, although Paul advised against it.

The early church had women leaders. Lydia was a founder of the church at Philippi. Although the early church had women leaders, it seems to have struggled to square the cultural presuppositions, the filters, about women with the experience of the gifts and leadership of women within the early congregations. Maybe the prominence of women by Luke is to assure the church where Theophilus, Luke's sponsor, is that the leadership of women can be traced all the way back to the apostles.

Not only was Lydia a woman but also she was a wealthy woman. Luke sounds a warning to the rich, but he never stereotypes the rich. Possessions do pose a danger but Luke doesn't lapse into divisive notions of class struggle. Jesus redeemed wealthy Zacchaeus. The parable of the Samaritan demonstrates the right use of wealth. Lydia demonstrates her commitment to God through hospitality.

When Paul consented to stay in Lydia's home and receive her hospitality, many barriers fell. Barriers that at the time divided male and female or divided Jew from Gentile or even divided Jew from Gentile Jewish convert and were within the synagogues did not hold in the church. In the Roman world, there was no movement out of the class into which one was born. But as Luke tells the story, specifically the chapter about Lydia, he draws a picture of relaxed familiarity and warm hospitality between social classes. This picture did not go unnoticed by Luke's readers in the first century. I suspect that you and I overlay this story with so many filters that we have had difficulty hearing or seeing the freedom that the followers of Christ experienced and practiced in the early church. And we have taken our cultural experiences and read them into the biblical story rather than permitting the biblical story to free us from these filters and blinders.

Lydia was a businesswoman who was open to God and was seeking more and more of God's love and grace in her life. As a result she became the first known businesswoman in the early church. Through the centuries Lydia has been an inspiration to many. I have a friend, Cheryl Collins Patterson, who lives in the Nevada desert with her physician husband. For several years Cheryl published a quarterly newsletter, *Lydia's Cloth*. The masthead is white lettering on a purple background. I share with you the purpose statement of the publication. "*Lydia's Cloth* is a newsletter written by women who serve in and through the Christian community. The purpose of *Lydia's Cloth* is to highlight the worship resources written by women; to provide a creative forum for traditional and alternative expressions of worship; to offer encouragement to those who are involved in planning worship for the Christian community." How creative! How historic! How prophetic! How appropriate!

Lydia's witness and her purple cloth inspired Cheryl to grow in faith, to seek God, and to develop her own witness through *Lydia's Cloth*. Will you permit this first-century businesswoman to inspire you? Will you permit Lydia's story to remove the filters from your eyes and ears so you may see and hear God's good news? What creative, prophetic, appropriate ministry will Lydia's witness and purple cloth inspire in you?

QUESTIONS TO PONDER

1. What intrigues you about Lydia?
2. What evidence do you see that indicates Lydia was a seeker?
3. How does your culture filter the way you read and hear Scripture?
4. What parallels do you see between your life and Lydia's life?
5. How can our understanding of Lydia contribute to shattering the stereotypes of women and men?
6. What characteristic do you see in Lydia that you would like to emulate in your life?

13

AN ETHIOPIAN SEEKER

ACTS 8:26–40

I DON'T KNOW HOW reading the Bible goes for you. I have heard many of the stories so often and heard certain emphases in particular stories so many times that I may not hear the significant impact of a particular story. For example, I had never thought of the Ethiopian eunuch as a person seeking God or being sought by God until I stumbled on this passage in Acts again during a time when I was formulating ideas for this book. This time, I found it extremely revealing, not only about the Ethiopian but also about me. I found it insightful and instructive for people in and out of the church today. However, I suspect many in the church will resist the insight and instruction revealed through the seeking experience of the Ethiopian eunuch.

It is customary on Mother's Day for many congregations in the United States to emphasize the importance of home and family. A lot is said today about family values. While family relationships are significant in our lives and contribute greatly to who we are, perhaps our culture tends to idolize family, at least a particular constellation of family. The tendency of congregations in recent years has been to define family as a father, a mother, and one and a half children. That definition omits everybody who has divorced. It omits blended families, single-parent families, singles, and friends who are mutually supportive and closer than any blood relatives ever thought of being. This approach omits seeing communal living as family. It certainly rejects homosexuals in committed relationships as family and does not consider significant others and unmarried people who live under the same roof as family.

Maybe there is no more cherished human arrangement than the family. We would die for our families. Some would even kill for their family. While many of us are not normally violent people, some would kill another person if necessary to save a family member's life. I know in many places, family ties are strong. Families become clans and to offend a member of an extended family is to offend the whole clan. People will come to the defense of their family no matter what the circumstances or evidence. The feud through the generations of the Hatfields and the McCoys in Kentucky may have become legendary, but there is a residue of that attitude in many families.

Thus the claim about kinfolk is often made that blood is thicker than water. After all, our family is the source of our identity, our name, and our values. Home, as one person said, is where they have to take you in. Family are the people who will take you in when everybody else has rejected you. There seems to be no limit to our love for our family. The church is praised as helping the family. Churches have "Family Night Suppers" and build "Family Life Centers." Congregations often seek to involve more people by advertising that they are a "Family Church."

As people look for a church, they often ask what the church has for their family. People often are seeking a full-service church for their family. Churches entice people to join them because "we have something for everybody." If we ever knew, we have forgotten how ambiguous the early church was about family. We have sought to make heaven over in our image and sing "may the circle be unbroken," forgetting that for Jesus the whole structure of relationships in the family of God is quite different from our understanding of family. Jesus said all are brothers and sisters to each other because are all children of God. This approach cuts across all bloodlines and weakens the claim that blood is thicker than water.

Wayne Meeks notes in *The First Urban Christians* that pagan Roman society had no more cherished value than its belief in the primacy of the family. Every Roman institution had its basis in the Roman family. There was no means of social advancement, other than the military, in ancient Rome other than marriage into a family, because your family determined your status in life.

We often fail to realize how many we exclude with this approach. There are those for whom *family* is not a positive word. There are those who do not define family the same way we do, and that creates distance.

As we learn more about family life and hear from people whose lives have been a mixture of joy and pain, achievement and struggle, we discover that family is the source not only of our greatest gifts, but also of our greatest damage. We have a tendency to expect the family to do everything for us, to bear too much moral and spiritual weight and to be all things to us. Families crack under the strain. Part of the reason for the family cracking is that we have too narrow of a definition of family. The culture and the church are often cohorts in crime as they load up the nuclear family with expectations that this nucleus of three or four or five people is to be everything and provide everything that those within the nuclear family need. The church needs to run counter to the culture. The church needs to help parents reassure their children that all the hopes, dreams, and aspirations the parents have are not resting on the child. The church can help parents and children alike recognize that the community of faith is a resource center for all of our lives and there are people in the church who are related to us by faith but not by blood who will help guard and guide us through life.

If you're not in a family, then you're apt to be very lonely, for we live in a society in which family is the most important attachment. And family in this situation has a rather narrow definition. Do you know of a church that builds a "Single Life Building"?

William Willimon remembers hearing a preacher in Duke Chapel preaching about Jesus' calling of his disciples, telling the story of inviting James and John, the sons of Zebedee, how they left their father holding the fishing nets and followed Jesus. The story doesn't say what their father thought about his two sons walking out of the family business and tagging along after the itinerant rabbi named Jesus. And the preacher commented, "Jesus broke the hearts of many a first-century family."[1]

Stanley Hauerwas opens one of his classes by reading a letter from a parent to a government official. The parent complains that his son, who had received the best education, gone to all the right schools, and was headed for a good job as a lawyer, had gotten involved with a weird religious sect. Now members of this sect controlled his every move, told him whom to date and whom not to date, and had taken all his money. The parent is pleading with the government official to do something about this weird religious group.

Who do you think the letter is describing? Does it sound like a group about whom you are suspicious? Does the letter express concerns and fears you have had?

It is a letter composed of several letters from third-century Roman parents concerning a group called the church. In the church's formation of a community of faith, it collided early with traditional, conventional definitions of family.

By now you may be wondering what any of this has to do with the story about an Ethiopian eunuch told to us by Luke in Acts. Well, for starters, the eunuch was not going to have a family as we "typically" define family. He was not going to have children or grandchildren. I think the passage in Acts 8: 26–40 raises some questions about our glorification of families and God's attempt to make a new "family" in the church. This new approach was evident during Jesus' ministry. You may recall the incident reported in the Gospels when Jesus' mother and brothers and sisters came for him and he asked those with whom he was talking, "Who is my mother and brother and sister?" Then Jesus answered by saying anyone who did the will of God was his mother or brother or sister. That was a new understanding of family. It is an understanding from which people have shied away through the centuries.

The order of events as portrayed in Acts is that it was five weeks after Easter when Philip met the Ethiopian eunuch. You do remember Easter, don't you? I know it has faded into the background. We tend to get back into our routines as soon after Easter as possible. The old boundaries have fallen back into place. The deadly boundaries seem so impervious, so impenetrable to the assaults of living. Some of the boundaries we love the most are those that provide us comfortable identity. We often don't realize how confined we are. Whether it is five weeks or fifty weeks after Easter, the tendency is the same. We tend to forget about resurrected lives, to forget what the whole meaning of God's work in Christ is all about. We settle back into our old routines, our old boundaries, and our old rules. Certain people are welcome and certain ones are "cut off."

Whenever angels appear in the book of Acts, something important is about to happen, a move is about to be made, a move so large that an angel, a special messenger from God, must be sent in to take charge. The move here is doubly weird, for it takes place in the desert, at noon, of all times.

The move being made by God is toward an "outsider," this Ethiopian of uncertain origin and orientation. Surely this is part of the Book of Acts program that the gospel shall be taken to "Jerusalem . . . Judea . . . Samaria, and to the end of the earth" (Acts 1:8). In the Greco-Roman world the term *Ethiopian* often applied to black people. The Ethiopians were considered exotic people who were from a faraway place. Their dark skin made them the object of wonder and admiration among Jews and Romans. They were considered to be from Timbuktu. They lived at the ends of the earth. The Ethiopian was a foreigner, a Gentile, one from about as foreign a place as existed. He was from as far on the other side of the tracks as anyone could ever be.

There was a second ostracizing characteristic about this man. He was a eunuch. It was common practice in those days for a king to have a male servant who had been castrated to manage his personal household. An added twist in this story is that the Ethiopian eunuch was the secretary of the treasury for Queen Candace of Ethiopia. Maybe his sexual status made it impossible for anyone to question the appropriateness of his relationship with the queen. While eunuchs often served in high places, everyone ostracized them. First, they had been ostracized by whoever made them eunuchs. The person in charge had said basically, "You cannot be trusted to act appropriately and with integrity and so you are being castrated." In this sense, eunuchs were guilty before the fact. They also were looked upon as weird, strange, bizarre people and the general population avoided having anything to do with eunuchs. They were treated as if they had some contagious, terminal disease. Not only did people keep their distance from them, but also they wrote rules and regulations that applied to them. It seems so easy for people in the majority or those in power to make rules that apply to other groups of people and in some way make those groups out to be enemies to be feared. And so, people feel cut off, ostracized, left out, and second class.

Of course, what often happens is that no one in the group completely fits the description. Who would have ever thought that a eunuch from the other side of the world would be interested in God? Surprise! Surprise! The Ethiopian eunuch already was a God-fearer. He was a seeker of God. He had been to Jerusalem to worship and while he may have worshiped God, he probably had to worship alone outside the Temple in the court of the Gentiles.

Philip is wandering along the road going down to Gaza from Jerusalem. In Israel, everything is down from Jerusalem. Philip catches a ride with the Ethiopian eunuch on his chariot. How fortunate for Philip! A chariot probably went by that place once every twenty or thirty years. Nevertheless, Philip got in the chariot and discovered that the eunuch was reading from the scroll of Isaiah. He had come to the passage that says: "He was led like a lamb to the slaughter, like a sheep before his shearers is dumb. He didn't open his mouth. Justice was denied him. He has been cut off from the land of the living. Who is going to declare his posterity?"

Who is going to declare his posterity! He will never have any posterity because he has been "cut off." He is without generation. He is cut off with no children to carry on the family name.

Just as soon as Philip gets into the chariot, the eunuch's first question is not "Who are you?" or "What are you doing way out here in the desert?" or "You sure are lucky I came along, aren't you?" His first comment is, "Who is that?" Who is that? Is the prophet talking about himself or someone else?

This man has been up to the Temple in Jerusalem but they wouldn't let him in. The Bible says clearly, "Don't let him in."

Why would anybody who went to church and was made to stand outside keep going to worship where he was not welcome? Why would he stand, all during the service, peering in, trying to get a hint of the music, hoping to hear just a snippet of the prayers? Standing on the outside, excluded, asking people in the crowds as they depart, "Was the sermon good today? What did the preacher say? What was the first anthem by the choir?"

Have you ever been to church, or been listening to Scripture, and had to stand outside?

In his exposition of this passage, Fred Craddock, Emeritus Professor of Preaching at Candler School of Theology, asks, "Why is this man so interested in this obscure, though beautiful, passage from Isaiah?"

And Craddock answers his own question. "I'll tell you why he is interested. He is a eunuch. The Scripture says quite plainly, as plain as the nose on your face, in Deuteronomy 21, 'The eunuch shall have no place in the congregation of the family of God.'" Talk about being cut off. How would you like to read in Scripture something that described a characteristic of yours and then added that nobody like this would ever have a place in the family of God? Well, just read the next verse in Deuteronomy after the verse about the eunuch. Here is what it says, "No one born to an unmarried woman or any descendant of such a person, even in the tenth generation, may be included among the Lord's people" (Deuteronomy 23:2). Now, I come from a pretty good family. Generally, they've been good, God-fearing people, but I'm sure if I went rummaging back through four hundred years of my ancestors I'd find at least one woman who had a child whose father was not her husband. So I'd be cut off, left out, no place for me in the congregational family of God.

There shall be no place in God's family for a eunuch. Why? Because it was all family oriented. He will never have a family, this sexless person, by accident, or choice, or royal decree. He will never have a family. Throughout Scripture, children are praised as a reward of God, a sign of divine favor. But this eunuch will never have children, will never have a family and therefore will have no place in the family of God. So the eunuch has a question, "Who is that?"

We are not told all that Philip said to the Ethiopian eunuch. I wonder if he urged him to read a little further in the scroll of Isaiah (56:3–5). Isaiah says that the days will come when the foreigner will no longer say, "The Lord will separate me from his people." The days will come when "to the eunuch who loves me and my house and my covenant I will give a name which shall be better than a thousand sons and daughters and will be remembered forever." Also in that passage Isaiah says, "A person who is a eunuch should never think that because he cannot have children, he can never be part of God's people." I wonder if Philip pointed to that passage and said, "Today this scripture has been fulfilled. Jesus of Nazareth has broken down every barrier and reinterpreted the entire meaning of the family of God. He has made a whole new family and it opens doors and knocks down walls in the family of faith like we have never seen nor heard." When the eunuch asked Philip, "Who is this to whom Isaiah is referring?" Philip replied, "Why, that was Jesus of Nazareth." "He was cut off. He had no family, no issue, and yet he created the largest family in the world."

This man from Ethiopia was seeking God and Philip introduced him to the understanding of God lived out and portrayed clearly in the life of Jesus. What excitement! What relief! One who thought that what had been done to him, because of his own choice or by the decree of another, had rendered him outside the pale of God's love and grace and acceptance found that was not true. The amazing grace and love of God were available to him as he sought to worship and serve God. He just knew that what had been done to him could not possibly have painted him outside the circle of God's love, and Philip said to this Ethiopian seeker, "You are exactly right. The love of God demonstrated in the life of Jesus draws a circle that includes everyone and you especially are included."

Right there in the middle of the desert, the eunuch asked to be baptized. Right there in the heat and the sand a white man and a black man, a Jew and an Ethiopian, Philip baptized the eunuch. And the eunuch became a member of a new family, the family of God, the largest family in the world. There he experienced water that unites; there he discovered that the water of baptism is thicker than blood when all along he had been told that blood was thicker than water. Is it not amazing how God is forever reversing the order of things because our order is usually exclusive and God's order of things is always inclusive?

If they sang a hymn before they went their separate ways, it must have gone something like O *Praise the Gracious Power*:

O praise the gracious power that tumbles walls of fear,
And gathers in one house of faith all strangers far and near;
REFRAIN: Praise Christ! Praise Christ! Whose cross has made
     us one!
O praise persistent truth that opens fisted minds,
And eases from their anxious clutch the prejudice that blinds.
     (Refrain)
O praise inclusive love, encircling every race,
Oblivious to gender, wealth, to social rank or place.
     (Refrain)
O praise the word of faith that claims us as God's own,
A living temple built on Christ, our rock and cornerstone.
     (Refrain)
O praise the tide of grace that laps at every shore
With visions of a world at peace, no longer bled by war.
     (Refrain)
O praise the power, the truth, the love, the word, the tide.
Yet more than these, O praise their source, praise Christ the crucified.
     (Refrain)[2]

The Ethiopian eunuch became a part of a "new" family, an enlarging, expanding group of people who were open and inclusive of all. What happened to the eunuch after this, we are not told. People in the early church held on to the tradition that he returned to Ethiopia and there shared the good news and found other seekers who joined with him as part of the body of Christ. Indeed that is what must happen to every seeker. Each of us who is seeking and being sought by God must align ourselves with others to be guarded and guided in our faith development. Never is a seeker after God portrayed in the Bible as a Lone Ranger. Never does a seeker go off only, completely, and totally by himself or herself. Development of faith happens in community.

Scott Russell Sanders discusses his research and reading into "efforts to re-establish bighorn sheep in the mountain and desert regions of the American West. Time and again, a goodly sized herd has been released into an area where bighorns once flourished, but then, year by year, their numbers dwindle away. The problem, it turns out, is that the sheep do not know how to move between their summer range and their winter range, and so they starve. Biologists can put the sheep in ideal habitat, can rig them with radio collars, can inoculate them against disease, but cannot teach them the migration routes that bighorns learn only from other bighorns. Once the link between sheep and ground is broken, and the memory of the trails is lost, there seems to be no way of restoring it."[3]

The bighorns die because they don't know where they are, and they don't know where they need to go. Churches languish and discipleship fades for the same reason. No matter how moving and profound our individual experiences of Jesus Christ as redeeming Savior may be, there needs to be more to see us through the duration of our lives. We need others, the community of faith, to guard us and guide us through all the changing scenery we will encounter in our lifetimes.

I appreciated a church member's observations and comments in a discussion group. Commenting about being actively involved in the West Jackson Baptist Church in Jackson, Tennessee, he made these comments that I paraphrase. "When I was growing up, my family attended the West Jackson Baptist Church. In all the years of my involvement in that church, I cannot remember attending a single youth activity. I do remember one youth activity that was canceled. It was a hayride and it was canceled when President Kennedy was killed. I can only remember one music presentation. It was the year the choir did *The Messiah* and the man who did the bass solo was awful. I don't remember any of the sermons that were preached. What I do remember are the people who constantly were there when I went to church. They served as models for me in my faith development. I think that's what we need to do. We need constantly to participate in the church, and in the process we will be models for others of faith development."

If you participate in a congregation, take a moment to think about the congregation with whom you worship. Are there some people in that congregation that you recognize as important guards and guides to your own faith? There probably are some you easily recognize—but others may not immediately catch your eye. But what you do recognize and remember are people who have included you regardless of who you were, what you had done, or what had been done to you. That was God's love and good news delivered through an angel. An angel is a messenger from God who delivers the message of God's good news of love and grace.

The Ethiopian eunuch is our brother the seeker who discovered that the love of God symbolized in the water of baptism is thicker than blood and more important than rules of exclusion. Whenever you have to choose between a relationship with a person and the keeping of a rule, choose the relationship every time. That's what Jesus did and it is what he calls us to do.

QUESTIONS TO PONDER

1. What is your definition of family?
2. Whom does your definition exclude?
3. Why was the Ethiopian eunuch drawn to the passage in Isaiah?
4. What enabled Philip to respond so positively to the Ethiopian eunuch?
5. Who are the people in our culture who are treated like the Ethiopian eunuch was treated?
6. What experiences have you had where you felt like you were treated like the eunuch was treated?
7. Who has been or could be Philip to you?
8. What needs to happen to you so you can respond to people who are "cut off" like Philip responded to the Ethiopian eunuch?

14

A NIGHT SEEKER

JOHN 3:1–21

"LIFE IS DIFFICULT," wrote Scott Peck in the opening line of his book *The Road Less Traveled*. Every one of us has experiences to support that statement but probably would change the wording to say, "Life is very difficult." Huge portions of our lives are spent in transition. We know very little about a settled existence. We are either just ending something or just beginning something. And it seems that there is a lot of disorder and chaos in between the endings and the beginnings. The Israelites finally were able to celebrate the ending of their enslavement in Egypt but they sure spent a lot of time wandering in the chaotic wilderness before they ever began their new life of freedom in the Promised Land. The majority of our years are spent in the chaotic wilderness between slavery and new life.

In the middle of the chaos the question "What does all of this mean?" becomes a gnawing, nagging question that will not leave us alone. People in every generation have asked it. They have asked it in a variety of ways. Always it is a seeker's question, the desire of one to get at the heart of life, to get at the meaning and purpose of living. In John's Gospel, when a seeker approaches

Jesus, John follows a pattern. The seeker says something. Jesus responds with a saying that is hard to understand. The seeker misunderstands the saying. Jesus responds with a saying that is even more difficult to understand. Then a discourse and explanation follow. John portrays people seeking, struggling, thinking things out, and discovering things for themselves. John uses this very pattern to tell the story of Nicodemus.

Most of our knowledge about Nicodemus is implicit rather than explicit. Nicodemus was a Pharisee, a Jewish leader, or ruler, and probably wealthy. In one sense the Pharisees were the best people in the whole country. There were never more than 6,000 of them. Pharisees took a vow in front of three witnesses to spend all their lives observing every detail of the scribal law, which was the first five books of Hebrew Scripture. This was considered to be the perfect word of God. It contained everything a person needed to know for living a good life. In order to live a good life there must be a rule and regulation to govern every possible moment of life. The Pharisees sought to extract rules and regulations from the great principles. In this endeavor, the Ten Commandments became over six hundred rules and regulations, often with legalistic interpretations. Jesus sought to summarize the six hundred rules and the Ten Commandments in two commandments.

The Pharisees had the responsibility of interpreting the meaning of Scripture for application in the lives of the Jews. For example, it was considered wrong to work on the Sabbath. The Pharisees were responsible to define what work was. To tie a knot on the Sabbath was interpreted as work and therefore wrong. But then, what constituted a knot? The knots that camel drivers and sailors tied were defined as work. It was also work to untie such a knot. Knots that could be tied or untied with one hand were legal. The Scribes worked out the regulations and the Pharisees dedicated their lives to keeping them. Pharisees were people who separated themselves from all ordinary life in order to keep every detail of the law. Nicodemus was a Pharisee.[1]

Nicodemus was also a Jewish leader or ruler. That means he was a member of the Sanhedrin. The Sanhedrin was an organization of seventy-one men who served as a supreme Jewish council in Jerusalem after the exile and until about 70 C.E. One of the duties of the Sanhedrin was to examine and deal with anyone suspected of being a false prophet. The Sanhedrin was a kind of religious Supreme Court.

As a practitioner of the Scriptures, Nicodemus was a teacher of religion, instructing people in the importance and value of relationship with God. He and apparently others were intrigued by Jesus because his introductory statement to Jesus was, "We know you are a teacher sent by God" (John 3:2). He and some of his colleagues must have been discussing what they had either heard about Jesus or observed Jesus doing or heard him say. Whether Nicodemus volunteered or was drafted to represent these people we have no way of knowing. However, even if he was drafted, Nicodemus probably felt a need to explore some things with Jesus. Usually the person who is willing to talk for another person about matters of concern feels those needs and concerns himself. Otherwise he would not be asked by others to represent them and his heart wouldn't be in it. The dialogue John recorded indicates Nicodemus' heart was in it.

Nicodemus went to see Jesus at night. This may have been a sign of caution. The fact that he went to see Jesus at all is amazing. However, the rabbis had declared the best time to study the Scriptures, the law, was at night when they would be undisturbed. Maybe Nicodemus wanted some private, undisturbed time with Jesus. Maybe he wanted Jesus to himself for an uninterrupted conversation.

Wonder what was happening in Nicodemus' life? For some reason life was not fulfilling for him. There was a void, an emptiness, a restlessness in his life that nagged him, and he thought that perhaps Jesus could help him with it. He knew that life had to have more meaning than he felt and he perceived that Jesus' dealings with other people had resulted in life getting better for them. Nicodemus was seeking, searching.

We are so much like Nicodemus. We have arrived at junctures in our lives and concluded that life had to have more value and meaning than we were experiencing. We have gone in search of meaning in life. One of the places to which many have turned is to the church. If ever there was a place where people might find an acceptable and helpful answer, often they conclude it might be in church. For many, church represents relationships, relationships with God and with people who are seeking to be in tune with God. We have come out of some loss, some ending in our lives and we are at loose ends as a result. Someone important has died, a relationship has died, disease has threatened us in a way we have never been threatened before, we have crossed over a dividing line in our lives and concluded there are some other things we want to do before our lives are over. Whatever it is, something has ended and nothing new has yet begun. We find ourselves in a neutral zone, a wilderness, where there seems to be no order and no direction. We flounder. We are in between. While we may not always put it in these words, we are in a faith crisis, a dangerous opportunity for faith to deepen or diminish. Ann Weems expresses it this way:

> Somewhere between the hurt and the heart
>   must come a decision
>   to reject
>   or cling to
>   the faith.
> Somewhere among the Why me?s and the anger
>   and the screaming No!s and the soft incessant
>   sobbing,
> Somewhere in the aching persistent pain
>   and the hopeless helpless nights,

Somewhere between the loud horror of what has
      happened
   and the quiet terror of silence
     comes
A turning away
    or a reaching out.
Somewhere between power and powerlessness
     comes
     the covenant cry
    and you either answer or you don't
    and you either live or you die.
"Therefore choose life,
    that you and your descendants may live."[2]

Nicodemus was somewhere between power and powerlessness. The covenant cry arose in him and he had either to live or to die. He sought out Jesus because he was seeking life.

How are you like Nicodemus? He is your brother, you know! And he is mine. He was a Pharisee. That means he knew the rules and lived by them. He was obedient. Religion was important to him. He took it seriously, maybe too seriously. I don't quite know why, maybe it's the way his questions are stated, but Nicodemus' face seems taut. He's just too rigid. And so are we. Again Ann Weems captures us, this time in her poem "The Lord of Life":

O Lord, we're playing Pharisee again,
   More interested in the Sunday morning count
     Than in the feeding of your sheep,
   More interested in the stars in our crowns
     Than in that cup of cold water,
   More interested in tradition and appearance
     Than in the following of our Lord.

O Jesus, you were real
And we made you saccharine and
        hung you on the church school wall
And told all the little children
        you wanted them to sit still.
O Jesus, you were here and now
And we made you something in the sweet by and by
And told all the people in need
        to see you in heaven.
O Jesus, you walked in our shoes in our marketplace
And we told you to stay in your sandals,
In a faraway place, in a long ago time,
        Stay back in the Bible.
O Jesus, we made you a baby that didn't cry,
        We made you a boy with good manners,
        We made you a man, sweet and gentle.
        We tossed you pennies,
        Then told you how to spend them.
        We built you temples,
        Then told you who could enter them.
        We made you wood and plastic and concrete
        And locked you in the church.
        We made you a goody-goody god
        And stood before the world with godless faces
                and pointing fingers
                        and tsk-tsk-tsk cold voices
                                declaring thou-shalt-nots.
O Lord! We paid no attention to Who You Are: the Lord of Life!
Jesus was into life
        in such a way
That you either had to follow him
        or resent his attempt to bring you change.

That's still who he is:
> Someone who's going to make you see yourself
> > if you have ears to hear.
O Lord, we're playing Pharisee again,
Playing at church
And making excuses about the real thing:
> Not me,
> Not now,
> Not with my income,
> Not with all I have to do . . .
Or making after-all speeches:
> After all, I give more than others I could name;
> After all, I do have five children;
> After all, I haven't been feeling well . . .
Or putting God off:
> As soon as we get the house paid for,
> As soon as we get the kids through college,
> As soon as we get this painting finished . . .
Christ was crucified for saying, Follow me now.
He was crucified for saying:
> You're storing up treasures
> Feed my sheep!
> You're blasphemers!
> Love God with everything you've got!
> And don't forget the cup of cold water!
Sweet and gentle? Meek and mild?
Christ came treading into our marketplaces, our
> temples, our homes—even into our private
> person—
> Teaching in the temple
> Preaching by the sea
> Questioning religious customs
> Breaking the ceremonial law
> Righting injustices

Healing the sick
Being joyful in the company of friends
Calling the children
Chiding good church members
Caring for unimportant people
Seeking out the sinners.
Christ came humbling himself,
Came loving the poor, the hungry, the lonely.
Christ came loving—
  This Lord of Life,
    This living, loving Lord.
O Lord, open our eyes to see the Pharisee within us.
Open our ears that we might hear the prophecy
Of the possibility of change.
Open the church doors that we might follow
  Our living, loving Lord
    Out into the marketplace.[3]

The Pharisee in Nicodemus and in us becomes so bound by the rules that we cannot receive or give love, grace, or mercy. Martin Luther wrote, "If I were as our Lord God and these vile people were as disobedient as they now be, I would knock the whole world in pieces" (*Table Talk*, CXI). It's a good thing Luther wasn't God! It's a good thing you and I aren't too!

Were we God, either we would shrink back and have nothing to do with the world or we would annihilate the world for not doing and being what we think the world should do and be. We have tried both approaches and stand on the brink of each today. We have isolated ourselves from others and said by our actions that their situations and needs are no concern of ours.

The Pharisee in Nicodemus and in us doesn't laugh. It's difficult for us to see anything funny. But laughter is the doorway for God to enter our lives. When we laugh, our defenses are down and God has the best chance of coming to us. Nicodemus heard

Jesus' response to him as humorous. Jesus told Nicodemus he needed to be born again. And Nicodemus chuckled as he said, "How can that be? How can a guy pushing sixty possibly pull that off? Is there some way that I can get back into my mother's womb and start life all over when I can't even get in a taxi without the driver coming around and giving me a shove from behind?"[4] And in the chuckle God got an entry way into Nicodemus' life and said, "Yeah, you do need to start all over, not by literally becoming a baby again but by having a whole new way of looking at life be born in you. You need to be born from above. Nicodemus, you need a completely new and different perspective on life."

Jesus said, "I'm telling you God's got such a thing for this loused-up planet that God sent me down so if you don't believe your own eyes, then maybe you'll believe mine, maybe you'll believe me, maybe you won't come sneaking around scared half to death in the dark any more but will come to, come clean, come to life."[5]

What Jesus said to Nicodemus was not a novel idea. It was not like no one had ever said such a thing before. Ezekiel had said it when he told his people that they could be sensitive and responsive to the needs of others but not as they were. Not with hard, cold, callous hearts. They must permit God to make them into new personalities with different, improved natures, with hearts of flesh, warm and sensitive. The Psalmist had expressed this same idea Jesus was offering to Nicodemus when he wrote, "Create in me a clean heart, O God; and renew a steadfast spirit within me" (Psalms 51:10). "Nicodemus," Jesus said, "are you a teacher of Israel and you don't understand this?" It wasn't the theory of new birth or being born from above that tripped Nicodemus but the sheer impracticality of it all.

What is, is, we conclude. But the whole point of the good news is that God can give us an entirely new understanding, perspective, way of looking and living. We've seen it happen in others' lives. We've experienced it to some extent in our own. Unpredictable, mysterious, new out of old, life out of death. God breaks into our lives but none of us ever guesses where or when or how.

And the whole purpose of God wanting to break into our lives is to give us a gift, the gift of love that translates into eternal life. The essence of eternal life has little to do with duration. Too few of us know what to do with this life much less what we would do with another one! Eternal life identifies not so much the length of a life as the kind of life. Eternal life identifies the ideal life, which is both present and future. It is authentic life that begins here and now but expands into the future and beyond this life into far greater existence. Even here and now we can experience eternal life but not completely. It is a quality of life that is peaceful, joyful, filled with hope. It is also in the future because life will widen, deepen, and expand.

William James, in his classic work *The Varieties of Religious Experience*, writes of "once-born" and "twice-born" people. The once-born are people who sail through life without ever experiencing anything that shatters or complicates their faith. They may have financial problems, disappointments with their children, but they never go through a time when they say, "The religion I was raised in is a lie; that's not how the world works." Their understanding of God when they are old is not that different from their view of God when they were children, a benign heavenly parent who keeps the world neat and orderly.

James's twice-born souls are people who lose their faith and then regain it, but their new faith is very different from the one they lost. Instead of seeing a world flooded with sunshine, as the once-born always do, they see a world where the sun struggles to come out after the storm but always manages to reappear. Theirs is a less cheerful, less confident, more realistic outlook. God is no longer the parent who keeps them safe and dry; God is the power that enables them to keep going in a stormy and dangerous world. And like the bone that breaks and heals stronger at the broken place, like the string that is stronger where it broke and was knotted, it is a stronger faith than it was before, because it has learned it can survive the loss of faith.[6]

God is love; a love that breaks through our understanding of what love is and runs out to lengths that sound incredible to us. "Love your enemies," God's love says. Jesus did. "Pray for those who despitefully use you." Jesus did. "If someone needs your coat, give him your shirt too." Jesus did. "If someone orders you to carry his load a mile, walk with him two." Jesus did. It really is possible. It can be done. People—real, live human beings—can be born again, born from above, completely changed from the inside out. Whatever words you use to describe what happens will be inadequate, but God's love for us is of such a nature that when we experience God's love, we have a totally different perspective on life. Life looks different to us. We live differently because we have been loved in a way we could not possibly imagine.

Nicodemus was a seeker who came to Jesus in search of understanding about the meaning and value of life. Jesus told him he needed a completely new perspective. He needed to be born from above. Like his first birth, this birth did not occur immediately or instantly but over a period of time and seasons in his life; the love and grace of God flowed freely to Nicodemus. Lo and behold he was changed from the inside out as God's love continued to touch new crevices in his life. Later when Jewish leaders wanted to condemn Jesus, Nicodemus intervened, reminding them that they were not to condemn anyone without first hearing what he teaches (John 7:50–52). Then, when Jesus was crucified and nearly all of the disciples were a frightened, scattered, hiding group, Nicodemus publicly joined Joseph of Arimathea in the broad daylight of Friday afternoon in asking for Jesus' body and preparing it for burial. He willingly stood as Christ's friend at the end to do what he could for the body to have a decent burial, the body of one despised by so many and considered as nothing more than pollution in the land. It probably was a crazy thing to do. After all, there was the fear that since they had come for Jesus, they would come for his disciples next and they wouldn't be too selective in identifying who was a disciple. But Nicodemus decided it was worth the risk. And the next day when Nicodemus heard that some of the disciples had seen Jesus alive again, he cried like a newborn baby.[7] As it was for Nicodemus, may it also be for you and me. Amen!

QUESTIONS TO PONDER

1. What is the Pharisee like in you?
2. What are the rules and regulations that you will keep at all costs?
3. Describe a recent event when you chose keeping a rule rather than relating to a person.
4. How are you like Nicodemus?
5. What does it mean to you to be born from above?
6. How would your life change if you were born from above?

15

THE SEEKER BEHIND ALL SEEKERS

HOSEA 2:1–3:5

I WONDER WHAT God's dream was in creating the world. What did God envision the creation to be like? When God dreamed of creating human beings, I wonder what God anticipated people would be like.

What do you think God's dream for you is? Do not misunderstand what I am asking. I am not suggesting that God had a mold that you were poured into when you were born and that you must stay in that mold all your life. I am not suggesting that God designed a meticulous plan for your life and if you can guess what it is, life will go well for you but if you don't guess correctly, life will be miserable.

God's vision or dream for us serves as a compass rather than a road map. A map has every intersection, every road, and every turn clearly indicated. Nothing is required of us but to get on the right road and follow the map. God's dream for us is much more like a compass. The magnetism of God's interest and concern for us draws us toward God. The direction of God's dream for us is toward relationship with God, but there are multiple routes we take to get there and multiple routes to travel in relationship with God. Composer Allen Pote expresses it this way:"O God remind us we are not alone. Though we move on different pathways, we are walking to your throne. Help us learn to love each other, show us ways to understand. We are members of one family, growing strong by joining hands."[1]

The greatest things parents can do for their children are provide a climate of love and acceptance that encourages the children to develop decision-making abilities, offer a variety of options for vocational consideration, and work with their children in discovering what their interests and abilities are. Then "train up" the children in the direction that their interests and abilities are going.

This is the way that God works with us. God invites us to focus on the gifts and abilities that are natural for us. We are to use these abilities to relate to and worship God, and we are to use these gifts and abilities to communicate God's care and presence for all of creation. Whenever we refuse or fail to do this, we blur God's vision and destroy God's dream for our lives. God's approach always is to guide us to refocus the vision and to dream again the dream God has for us. Apparently, as long as there is life in a person there is the possibility that God can resurrect in that person the dream God had for the person.

A story will help us better comprehend this. The story is about a woman named Gomer. Isn't that a strange name for a woman, for anyone—Gomer? The only Gomer with which many of us are familiar is Gomer Pyle. We smile because he was a television character portrayed as a buffoon. We laughed at his expense. The name Gomer has a humorous, but negative association for us.

Gomer is a unisexual name. In Genesis (10:2–3) Japheth had a son named Gomer. In the biblical book named Hosea we are told that the leading character, Hosea, married a woman named Gomer. It is amazing how reputations are associated with names. A person who has a negative reputation seldom has people named for her. Even those who like the sound of the name have not named their daughters Gomer because of the reputation of the wife of Hosea.

I think the best way to get a grasp on Gomer's story is to let Frederick Buechner tell it in modern fashion. Here is how Buechner describes Gomer and her activities.

Gomer was always good company—a little heavy with the lipstick maybe, a little less than choosy about the men and booze, a little loud, but great at a party and always good for a laugh. Then the prophet Hosea came along wearing a sandwich board that read "The End is at Hand" on one side and "Watch Out" on the other.

The first time he asked her to marry him, she thought he was kidding. The second time she knew he was serious but thought he was crazy. The third time she said yes. He wasn't exactly a swinger, but he had a kind face, and he was generous, and he wasn't all that crazier than everybody else. Besides, any fool could see he loved her.

Give or take a little, she even loved him back for a while, and they had three children whom Hosea named strange names like Not-Pitied and Not-My-People because God will no longer pity Israel now that it has gone to the dogs. So every time the roll was called in school, Hosea would be scoring a prophetic bullseye in absentia. But everybody could see the marriage wasn't going to last, and it didn't.

While Hosea was off hitting the sawdust trail, Gomer took to hitting as many night spots as she could squeeze into a night, and any resemblance between her next batch of children and Hosea was purely coincidental. It almost killed him, of course. Every time he raised a hand to her, he burst into tears. Every time she raised one to him, he was the one who ended up apologizing.

He tried locking her out of the house a few times when she wasn't in by five in the morning, but he always opened the door when she finally showed up and helped get her to bed if she couldn't see straight enough to get there herself. Then one day she didn't show up at all.

He swore that this time he was through with her for keeps, but of course he wasn't. When he finally found her, she was lying passed out in a highly specialized establishment located above an adult bookstore, and he had to pay the management plenty to let her out of her contract. She'd lost her front teeth and picked up some scars you had to see to believe, but Hosea had her back again and that seemed to be all that mattered.

He changed his sandwich board to read "God is love" on one side and "There's no end to it" on the other, and when he stood on the street corner belting out:

> *"How can I give you up, O Ephraim!*
> *How can I hand you over, O Israel!*
> *For I am God and not man,*
> *The Holy One in your midst."* (Hosea 11:8–9)

Nobody can say how many converts he made, but one thing that's for sure is that, including Gomer's there was seldom a dry eye in the house."[2]

That's quite a love story, isn't it? It's not your predictable modern-day romance novel or television soap opera. This was a dark tragedy in Hosea's life. As he agonized over his experience with Gomer and the way she had related to him, or hadn't related, had rejected him and gone off to do her own thing, Hosea began to sense a faint reflection in what Gomer had done to him of what people, especially the people of Israel, had done to God. No one in Israel had ever suggested before that the way lovers related to each other was an analogy of the way God and human beings relate to each other. This marked a turning point in the Bible in the understanding of how God feels toward human beings and what it is to sin. Sin as portrayed through Hosea's experience with Gomer is to blur the vision and kill the dream God has for relating to people, to betray the central relationship of one's being.

Hosea's relationship with Gomer gave him a whole new way of reviewing Israel's history. Israel had been an unfaithful bride of this God called Yahweh. God went to this slave people in Egypt who were "no people" and delivered them from their plight. In the desert at Sinai, God had "married" the nation Israel and promised to care and provide for them with abundant affection, and they in turn were to prefer God above all others and to have no other lover-gods besides Yahweh. But God's experience with Israel was like Hosea's experience with Gomer. The people of Israel had just barely settled in their new home and were experiencing more love and provision than ever when they began going after the gods of Canaan. They deserted God as surely as Gomer had abandoned Hosea and their children.

For some reason Hosea kept reaching out to Gomer, seeking her, wanting to take her back. In the middle of this tragic relationship and Hosea's urge to reach out to Gomer, he began to understand that the reason he felt the way he did toward Gomer was actually the image of a God of everlasting mercy rising up within him. As surely as Hosea was seeking Gomer, Hosea realized that God was seeking him, all of Israel, and all people for that matter.

This chapter about Hosea summarizes all the other chapters and basically is the underpinning for all of them. Behind all of Hosea's seeking was God seeking people. God is the seeker behind all our seeking. Because of this awareness of God, Hosea moved out in sacrificial love to attempt to restore what was fallen and broken. Through his own tragedy, Hosea saw more clearly than anyone up to that time that sin blurs our vision of God and kills God's dream in us. He saw that God truly is a God of mercy who keeps reaching out to people, seeking to guide them in refocusing their vision and giving them the grace and forgiveness they need to dream again their relationship with God.

God's dream for Gomer was that she be a person of love and tenderness toward others, especially toward her husband and children. God wanted her to be a person who could be trusted and counted on as a loyal and faithful friend, wife, and mother. For whatever reasons, and the causes are multiple, Gomer blurred God's vision of her and destroyed God's dream of her life by being untrustworthy, disloyal, and unfaithful. Our attitude and approach would often be, "Let her go. Forget about her. She's had enough chances to change. Don't waste your time on her. She never will change."

But God's way of relating is quite different. Usually through some human relationship, God seeks anyone who has blurred the vision of what it means to be a child of God. In this case it was through her husband, Hosea, that God sought to reach Gomer. Through this process Hosea caught the vision and lived the dream of what God is like and how God relates.

Hosea discovered both the destructive power of sin and the greater recreative power of God's mercy. Sin is more than the breaking of a law; it is the betrayal of the tender bond of love. Hosea easily could have been done with Gomer. Instead, at a cost far greater than silver and barley, he set out through suffering love to woo and win her again as God was doing and had been doing over and over again through the centuries with the people of Israel. What was portrayed as God wooing the Israelites was a metaphor of what God had been doing and continues to do with all people everywhere.

We often portray God in a judgmental fashion and imply that God is waiting to do us in because of some wrong we have done. We are accountable to God for our lives. God does not take lightly our betrayal of the tender bond of love we have with God.

But motivated out of infinite love and tender mercy to reach over the worst we have done and draw us into relationship, God seeks us. I find it difficult to grasp the idea that God is willing to take me back after I have been openly disloyal, unfaithful, and untrustworthy. If a friend of mine were to betray me and then want to reestablish the friendship, I think I would be able to work through my anger and disgust and be friends again. But if this friend did this time and time again, I'm not sure I have it in me to keep reestablishing the relationship. I know I have it in me to be outraged at such a proposal and to refuse to relate on anything but a superficial level, if I were to relate at all.

Yet, God continually is seeking us. God is willing, even eager, to accept us back even when we have shown that we prefer anything and everything else to our relationship with God. C. S. Lewis has stated this powerfully.

> It is a poor thing to strike our colors to God when the ship is going down under us; a poor thing to come to Him as a last resort, to offer up 'our own' when it is no longer worth keeping. If God were proud, He would hardly have us on such terms. But He is not proud; He stoops to conquer! He will have us even though we have shown that we prefer everything else to him, and come to Him because there is nothing better now to be had. . . . It is hardly a compliment to God that we should choose Him as an alternative to Hell; yet even this He accepts.[3]

This image of God's mercy is incredible and we need to open ourselves to it again and again. We need to proclaim it again and again. But our tendency is to ignore God. To ignore means to be ignorant, not to know, to have no knowledge of a subject or situation. Sometimes we ignore God because we are convinced that God is nowhere to be found. Other times we ignore God because we are ashamed to admit what we have done or we are convinced of how God must feel about us. We conclude there is no way God could accept us because we cannot accept ourselves. Look at the damage we've done. Look at the blurred vision and the dead dream we have made of our lives.

I read of a movie actress who said she would not "have the nerve" to approach God anymore. She had been raised in a strong religious atmosphere, but she confessed that she had been so enamored with success and so busy in her profession that she had not given God a thought for twenty years. She concluded: "I would not have the gall now to pray. Heaven knows how He must feel about me now, seeing how I have neglected Him so long."

This is a logical conclusion except for one thing. This is not the way God relates. It may describe the way we relate or how we would respond if we were ignored for a year or twenty, but it is not the way God relates. Not only is God eager and willing to take us back, but also it is God who is working with us, seeking to initiate our return. God's everlasting mercy is astonishing!

Wherever you are in your journey today, whatever you have done to blur God's vision and kill God's dream in your life, I want you to realize that in the everlasting mercy of God there always is welcome, always the possibility of return. As long as there is life in us, it is possible for God to refocus the vision and reshape the dream that God has for us.

We can start by stopping. We must stop ignoring God and acknowledge that God is present in our lives seeking to woo and win us back into relationship. There is nothing too major for God to handle and forgive. There is no one so unlovely or unlovable that God cannot and will not love and accept. God's mercy is astonishing and everlasting and only our ignorance, our ignoring God, will blur the vision and kill the dream of life, love, peace, and joy that come through God's mercy, forgiveness, and acceptance of us. Catch the vision of God's mercy, live the dream of God's forgiveness, and permit God to refocus the vision and reshape the dream of a loving relationship with you.

What a seeker God is! What awe to be sought by God! What joy to permit God to find us! Indeed, the seeker behind all seekers and all our seeking is a loving, forgiving, caring, merciful friend we call God.

QUESTIONS TO PONDER

1. How are you like Gomer? In what ways have you continually rejected God?

2. Who have been the Hoseas in your life?

3. Reflect on your life. Identify at least one time when God was seeking you. What was happening in your life? How was God seeking you? How did you respond? What was exciting and invigorating about that? What was troubling and frightening about that?

4. When have you been Hosea to someone? What events led up to you being Hosea to someone? How did that person respond to your efforts? Did you give up? If so, why? If you did not give up, what enabled you to continue being Hosea to that person?

5. Reflecting on the story of Hosea and Gomer, what have you learned about God, yourself, and your relationship with God?

NOTES

CHAPTER 1
1. Edward P. Wimberly, *African American Pastoral Care* (Nashville: Abingdon Press, 1991), 57.
2. Clyde Fant (sermon delivered at Stetson University, Deland, FL, n.d.).
3. Ibid.

CHAPTER 2
1. David Steele, "The Jacob Cycle," *Theology Today* 37, no. 4 (January 1981): 461–62.
2. Ibid.

CHAPTER 3
1. Steele, "The Jacob Cycle," 469.
2. Ibid., 470.
3. Ibid.

CHAPTER 4
1. Frederick Buechner, *Peculiar Treasures: A Biblical Who's Who* (San Francisco: Harper and Row, 1979), 65.
2. Victor Frankl, *Man's Search for Meaning* (New York: Washington Square Press, 1963), 104.
3. John Killinger, *For God's Sake, Be Human* (Waco: Word Books, 1970), 139.
4. Philip Yancey, *Disappointed with God* (New York: HarperPaperbacks, 1991), 173.
5. Ibid., 185–86.
6. C. S. Lewis [N. W. Clerk, pseud.], *A Grief Observed* (London: Faber and Faber, 1961), 9.
7. Yancey, *Disappointed with God*, 285.
8. Buechner, *Peculiar Treasures*, 65.

9. John Claypool, "The Alchemy of God" (sermon delivered at Northminster Baptist Church, Jackson, MS, 22 March 1981).

10. Yancey, *Disappointed with God*, 243–44.

CHAPTER 6

1. Welton Gaddy, "Help in a Cemetery" (sermon delivered at Broadway Baptist Church, Ft. Worth, TX, 14 August 1983), 1.

CHAPTER 7

1. Quoted in Steve Hyde, "Facing Our Fear of . . . Stewardship" (sermon delivered at First Baptist Church, Silver Spring, MD, 13 November 1988), 1.

2. Ibid., 2.

CHAPTER 8

1. I am indebted to colleague Linda Weaver-Williams for many of the insights about the dialogue between Jesus and the Syrophoenician woman.

CHAPTER 9

1. Buechner, *Peculiar Treasures*, 180.

2. *Homiletics* 1, no. 4 (October–December 1989), 20.

3. Buechner, *Peculiar Treasures*, 181.

CHAPTER 11

1. Boris Pasternak, *Doctor Zhivago* (New York: Pantheon Books, 1997), 397.

2. George A. Buttrick, ed. *The Interpreter's Bible Commentary* 9 (Nashville: Abingdon Press, 1952), 839.

3. L. D. Johnson, *Introduction of the Bible* (Nashville: Broadman Press, 1964), ix.

4. Ibid., 843.

CHAPTER 13

1. William Willimon, "When Water Is Thicker Than Blood," *Pulpit Resource* 22, no. 2 (South St. Paul: Logos Productions, April–June 1994), 22.

2. Thomas H. Troeger, "O Praise the Gracious Power," *The Baptist Hymnal* (Nashville: Broadman Press, 1991), 226.

3. Scott Russell Sanders, "Telling the Holy," *Parabola* 18 (May 1993): 8–9.

CHAPTER 14

1. William Barclay, *The Daily Bible Study Series, The Gospel of John*, 1 (Philadelphia: Westminster Press, 1956), 109–11.

2. Ann Weems, *Family Faith Stories* (Philadelphia: Westminster Press, 1985), 50.

3. Ann Weems, *Reaching for Rainbows* (Philadelphia: Westminster Press, 1980), 26–28.

4. Buechner, *Peculiar Treasures*, 122.

5. Ibid.

6. Reported by Harold Kushner, *Who Needs God* (New York: Summit Books, 1989), 41.

7. Buechner, *Peculiar Treasures*, 123.

CHAPTER 15

1. Words and music by Allen Pote, *Many Gifts, One Spirit* (Bryn Mawr, PA: Coronet Press, Theodore Presser, Selling Agent, 1987).

2. Buechner, *Peculiar Treasures*, 43–44.

3. C. S. Lewis, *The Problem of Pain* (New York: Macmillan, 1962), 97.

BIBLIOGRAPHY

BOOKS

Barclay, William. *The Daily Bible Study Series, The Gospel of John*, 1. Philadelphia: Westminster Press, 1956.

Buechner, Frederick. *Peculiar Treasures: A Biblical Who's Who*. San Francisco: Harper and Row, 1979.

Buttrick, George A., ed. *The Interpreter's Bible Commentary*. 12 vols. Nashville: Abingdon Press, 1952.

Frankl, Victor. *Man's Search for Meaning*. New York: Washington Square Press, 1963.

Johnson, L. D. *Introduction of the Bible*. Nashville: Broadman Press, 1964.

Killinger, John. *For God's Sake, Be Human*. Waco: Word Books, 1970.

Kushner, Harold. *Who Needs God*. New York: Summit Books, 1989.

Lewis, C. S. [N. W. Clerk, pseud.]. *A Grief Observed*. London: Faber and Faber, 1961.

———. *The Problem of Pain*. New York: Macmillan, 1962.

Weems, Ann. *Family Faith Stories*. Philadelphia: Westminster Press, 1985.

———. *Reaching for Rainbows*. Philadelphia: Westminster Press, 1980.

Wimberly, Edward P. *African American Pastoral Care*. Nashville: Abingdon Press, 1991.

Yancey, Philip. *Disappointed with God*. New York: HarperPaperbacks, 1991.

PERIODICALS

Craddock, Fred. "Living by the Word." *The Christian Century* 107, no. 8 (7 March 1990).

Homiletics 1, no. 4 (October–December 1989): 20.

Sanders, Scott Russell. "Telling the Holy." *Parabola* 18 (May 1993): 8–9.

Steele, David. "The Jacob Cycle." *Theology Today* 37, no. 4 (January 1981): 461–62.

Willimon, William. "When Water Is Thicker Than Blood." *Pulpit Resource* 22, no. 2 (South St. Paul: Logos Productions, April–June 1994): 22.

MUSIC

Pote, Allen. "Many Gifts, One Spirit." Bryn Mawr, PA: Coronet Press, Theodore Presser, Selling Agent, 1987.

Troeger, Thomas H. "O Praise the Gracious Power." *The Baptist Hymnal.* Nashville: Broadman Press, 1991.

SERMONS

Claypool, John. "The Alchemy of God." Sermon delivered at Northminster Baptist Church, Jackson, MS, 22 March 1981.

Fant, Clyde. Sermon delivered at Stetson University, Deland, FL, n.d.

Gaddy, Welton. "Help in a Cemetery." Sermon delivered at Broadway Baptist Church, Ft. Worth, TX, 14 August 1983.

Hyde, Steve. "Facing Our Fear of . . . Stewardship," Sermon delivered at First Baptist Church, Silver Spring, MD, 13 November 1988.

A STORY TO LIVE BY

KATHY GALLOWAY

0-8298-1334-9/paper/144 pages/$16.95

Galloway uses her experience to help us contemplate three basic questions. What is my story? What has helped shape my story? and How does my story relate to the stories of others? Drawing on her extensive knowledge of Celtic spirituality and her deep sense of social justice, she address such themes as the search for roots, the role of work, and the need of values.

**To order call The Pilgrim Press
1-800-537-3394**